Tomorrow's Troubles

Betty B. Robison

WinePress Publishing
MUKILTEO, WA 98275

Tomorrow's Troubles
Copyright © 1997 by Betty B. Robison

Published by:
Winepress Publishing
PO Box 1406
Mukilteo, WA 98275

Cover by **DENHAM**DESIGN, Everett, WA

Printed in the United States of America

ISBN 1-57921-024-4
Library of Congress Catalog Card Number: 97-60733

CONTENTS

CHAPTER ONE

TODAY IS NOW

It was a hot day in August. I was four years old and didn't yet know the meaning of "Dust Bowl," even though I lived in one. Barefoot, brown, squinting in the sun—I was happy in my own dream world, completely unaware of soaring temperatures. It was a normal summer heat. The sounds around me were gentle: an occasional squeaking of the windmill when a casual breeze strayed by and caught in its wheel, or the lazy clucking of a few chickens as they pecked in the dirt.

This private moment of *now* was all mine. I wished a ladybug would fly down on my hand and say, "Come with me and see my house and my babies." I'd go, of course. I don't think I'd even ask Mama first. Maybe I would tell her about it later, though. I wondered what a ladybug's house looked like.

"Bonnie May, come in here and get washed for dinner." Mama's voice erased my dream and I kicked up some dust as I skipped into the house. My cousin, Barbara Jean, and I had recently learned to skip. It was a lot more fun than running. Sometimes I stubbed my toe, but that didn't matter in the dust.

"You want to bake your brains?" Mama scolded. "It's 110 in the shade today and you stand out there in the hot sun. Now hurry and wash so you can help me set the dinner table before Daddy comes in."

Dinner was our noon meal. Mama said we were mighty lucky to have three square meals a day—breakfast, dinner and supper. I sometimes wondered what a square meal was and if some people had other kinds.

I went to the washstand in the corner of the kitchen and carefully dipped my hands in the pan of water Mama had set there for me. It might be too hot and I wouldn't want to burn myself. It was just a nice, middle-sized warm and I tried putting in my whole hand, then my arms. The pan wasn't big enough to reach my elbows. I watched the water change to a brownish color as some of the dirt floated off.

"Mama, what's brains?" I thought I knew but wasn't sure.

"They are what you think with."

"Where are they?"

"In your head."

"Does everybody have some?"

"Yes…well, most everybody I suppose. Unless they stood in the sun too long and baked them." She smiled and I knew that must have been her joke. I wasn't worried, though, because I remembered that I had been thinking about ladybugs and so I must still have had some brains.

"If you don't hurry and get the table set, I'll have to do it and then you can't tell Daddy how you helped me today," Mama threatened. That really got me started. I loved to brag to Daddy about how good I was. I adored him and wanted to make sure he felt the same way about me. I had a baby brother who kept Mama quite busy, so I spent as much time as I could with Daddy—when he wasn't working in the field or doing chores around the farm, that is.

I hastily wiped the rest of the dirt from my hands on the towel and began arranging the plates and knives and forks on the bright new oilcloth. New oilcloth had a special pleasant smell. This one was white with red apples and green stems all over it. I decided that when I learned to count some more—I could count to fifteen—I would count all the apples to see how many there were. Barbara Jean said a *jillion* is about as high as numbers go. *Wonder if there could be a jillion apples on our tablecloth?*

Then Daddy came in, kissed Mama, hugged me and went to the washpan to wash. "Something dirty fell in this water," he laughed. Mama brought him fresh water from the teakettle.

I liked our dinners. We usually had fried potatoes and I got to eat as much of the crispy part as I liked. Today we had pork chops and creamed dried corn and sliced tomatoes from the garden. There was always homemade bread and churned butter, and a tall glass of cool milk which Mama had just brought up from the cellar. There was chocolate cake for dessert—my favorite.

Daddy ended his dinner with some soppin' molasses. He poured molasses on his plate, dropped a hunk of butter in the middle and stirred with a spoon until it was light and creamy. Then he sopped it up on the half piece of bread he had saved. He liked that better than dessert. Sometimes I felt I ought to like it too, but molasses made me gag. Mama said it did her too. But Daddy just smiled and ate it like it was chocolate cake. His plate was so clean when he got through, I didn't know why we had to wash it for supper.

Daddy told us that Uncle Bob had come by the field on his way over to the Foster farm where he was going to work for a few days. "What did he have to say?" Mama always asked that.

"Well, not much. Except that Turner's old mare fell in the well and died, and the post office has a new revolving door, and we are all invited over to Grandma's for dinner after church Sunday."

Mama thought that was quite a bit of news, but I heard only part of it. "What is a 'volving door, Daddy?"

"Oh," he said, "It's really like three doors fastened together that go around and around. You walk in between them."

"Do you get caught in between them?" I asked.

"No, you just have to watch when you step in and when you step out, or you might have to go around more than once. It's kind of like jumping rope."

This was a brand new thing. I was curious and thought I really must see this revolving door. For several days I tried to picture it in my mind. I imagined myself walking up those post office steps, taking a look at the door and stepping in at just the right time and out at just the right time. Everyone would be admiring me because I was so young and so brave. Well, maybe I wouldn't go in it the first time. Maybe I'd just stand outside while Daddy or Mama went in to mail a letter and watch all the people go round and round in that door.

"Revolving door…" I practiced saying it. Then I drew a circle in the dirt with a stick and practiced walking around in it. One side was for stepping in and one side for stepping out. Just then Mama looked out the window and she didn't see the lines I had drawn. But she saw me, walking in little circles. I guess she thought I did bake my brains because in her worried voice she said, "Child, what are you doing?"

I told her I was just playing revolving doors, and she laughed and said, "You and your imagination! I declare you're going to be a writer or a movie star some day." I saw a picture show once with my aunt. I said I'd rather be a movie star because they were so beautiful and got to wear high heels. Anyway, I didn't know what a writer was. *It must be someone who knows how to write.* I'd learn that next year when I started to school. Perhaps I'd be both a writer and a movie star.

One morning at breakfast, Daddy said he had to go in to town. I heard Mama say, "Why don't you stop at the post office and get some stamps? I'll write a letter to Ellen." Aunt Ellen lived in Cincinnati. Daddy promised he would and said he'd be leaving as soon as he finished the chores.

The post office! My brains really started working! I had to see that revolving door. It wouldn't do to ask to go along because Mama was making me a new dress for Sunday, and I knew she wanted to try it on me and put pins in the hem. Saying, "Scuse me, please," I got up from the table, trying to act very natural.

I went out the door and kicked up a little dust as I skipped to my playhouse at the side of our house. It was only a place with the rooms marked off with a stick. There was an old bench by the side of the house for a table and a box with some broken dishes in it for a cupboard. From my playhouse I could crawl under the side porch. That was my storm cave in case of cyclones. There were some pretend children made out of corn husks and string. Mama had sewed some buttons on for eyes. *I must get them up out of their shoebox bed and tell them to wash for breakfast.*

I told them I had to go to town that day and they were to mind the house while I was gone. It was just play talk, but I kept thinking; and the more I thought, the more important it seemed to go to town to see that revolving door. There wasn't always a line between my pretend world and the real world. They blended together for me. I was happy with that.

I sat down by my play table and waited. After awhile I saw Daddy come back into the house from the barn. Then I ran to the car shed. I made sure not to stir up any dust this time. I opened the door just a little. It slid on some kind of a track from side to side and it wasn't hard for me to open just enough to get through. Then I closed the door and climbed into the car. On the floor of the back seat there was a pile of gunny sacks which I squirmed under, making sure I was well covered.

Soon Daddy came out and opened the shed door, cranked the car, got in and we were on the road to town. He hadn't even looked in the back seat. I was finally on my way to see the amazing revolving door. I liked the word *amazing*. It must be a good word to describe a revolving door.

When we got to town and the car stopped, I was especially careful to lie quietly. I wasn't going to spoil my plan now. Daddy got out and I heard him walk away. It seemed so quiet all around that I didn't think we could be downtown, so I peeked out the window. We were at my grandmother's house. I scooted back down and covered up again. In a few minutes Daddy came out and cranked the car to start it. Then he got in. Grandmother must have come flying out of the house because I heard her yell, "Wait, wait—William, wait!"

She came out to the car and said rather breathlessly, "Mary just called and said that she can't find Bonnie May anywhere. She wondered if she came with you." I was very still. My Daddy said in his worried voice, "No, she didn't. I wonder where she could be."

Just then, my grandmother looked in the back window and I heard her say to Daddy, "What is that lump under those gunny sacks on the floor?"

Uh-oh.

Of course I came up then—very dusty, hot and sweaty and really scared I'd get a spanking. But Daddy didn't even scold me. He and Grandmother were both glad to see me, I guess. Daddy thanked Grandmother for the stamps she loaned him. We left and Grandmother went in the house to call Mama.

After I got home that day and discovered that I wasn't going to be punished, I told Mama and Daddy why I went to town. I wanted to see the revolving door. They both laughed and Daddy said, "Well, you'll get to see it one of these days." And I did, the next week. I walked through the door when we mailed the letter to Aunt Ellen. Then I walked back out through it. Somehow, it didn't seem like much. That was when I found that sometimes thinking about a thing can be bigger than doing it.

The moments I called "now" were for the most part happy moments. Some of the simplest things added to

11

the happiness. Things like having neighbors in for an evening visit. When there were other children, we were allowed to play outside in the dark. I learned all about catching fireflies. We called them *lightning bugs*. We put them in a jar and watched them light up the jar in the dark. Sometimes we had a contest to see who could catch the most and put them in separate jars.

At first I didn't catch many, but with a little practice I began getting my share. They are rather slow and not hard to catch. Before we tired of the game, Mama called, "You children want some pie and milk? Come on in." We let all the lightning bugs go so they could light up the yard. No one saved them because they don't light in the day time. Some of the older children would squeeze the light off and put it on their fingers to make glowing rings. I hated that because I didn't like killing the friendly little bugs and, besides, I couldn't stand squishing anything.

One of the exciting "now" moments was a day when Daddy let me go with him to the field. He said he had to take the wagon out to an old barn across the north field to bring back some hay. Mama put a faded sunbonnet of Grandma's on my head to keep the sun from "beating down too hard." Daddy had on his straw hat with a kerchief tied around his neck. I never knew why they worried so much about the sun.

Sitting up on that springboard wagon seat behind old Prince and Dolly, I felt as important as the Queen of Sheba. Barbara Jean said the Queen of Sheba was probably the most important woman in the world. I didn't know if that was true, but saying "Queen of Sheba" made us sound grown up. We talked about her a lot—mostly made up stories.

Daddy asked me if I would like to drive the team, and I'll tell you I felt *more* important than the Queen of Sheba. I'll bet she never got to do anything like that, especially when she was a little girl. Daddy handed me the reins and I grabbed them with all my might and said, "Whoa!" Those surprised horses stopped pretty fast.

Daddy said, "Why did you do that?"

"You told me I could drive and I wanted to see if it worked when I yelled 'Whoa.'" I smiled with satisfaction, enjoying the unusual sense of power.

Daddy chuckled, "All right, now what are we going to do?"

I still held on tightly but tried to give the horses' backsides a little slap with the lines the way Daddy does. I said, "Giddyap!" Nothing happened. My power experiment was over. Daddy took the reins and got the horses started.

"For now," he said, "why don't you just practice holding the reins. Not too tight now. That's right, and I'll help with the starting and stopping and turning. That takes a little more experience." So I did what he said, and we got there much too soon to suit me.

While Daddy was loading the hay in the wagon, I went over to the fence and picked up hedge apples. Many of the fields in Kansas had hedgerows growing along the fence. I didn't know what they were for, but most children had played catch with the fruit from them. It was not really fruit. Mama said it was poison and we were to wash our hands after we had played with them. They were very hard and larger than eating apples. I piled up some of them to use for pretend snowballs and threw some at the fence. I wasn't very good at throwing. Some things boys can do better than girls. Throwing is one of those things.

I heard a rumble of thunder and stopped to look up at the sky. The sun had almost disappeared behind some dark rolling clouds. Daddy called me and said we'd better start back because that cloud had wind and hail in it. He was always right about the weather. As he helped me into the wagon, the wind blew the tail of my sunbonnet and I felt a large drop of rain on my nose.

I didn't even ask who would drive home. I wanted to get there in a hurry. I didn't like storms. Soon the horses were galloping down the road and we were bouncing around on that wagon seat with rain splashing all over us. About halfway home, the hail started coming down—just tiny little ones about the size of peas, at first. But they kept getting bigger and bigger.

As we pulled into the barn, Daddy said, "I guess we got home just in time. I was about to put you under the seat so the hail wouldn't knock you off." When we looked out the barn door, we saw hailstones as big as hedge apples lying on the ground. Daddy said he had never seen any so large before.

The storm didn't last long, and we were soon in the house getting dried off and talking about our experience. From the comfortable kitchen, as we looked out at the clearing sky, it seemed we had just had a very wonderful and exciting adventure. I could hardly wait to tell Barbara Jean about it. She got to ride on an elephant once when a circus came to town and I didn't. I could forgive her for that now, because I bet she never drove a team of horses or rode in a wagon in a hailstorm.

Our days on the farm were happy days; but the next year, for some reason I didn't understand, my parents decided to move into town. My father was going to give up our kind of farming and work with my grandfather who was a vegetable farmer. We would be living half a block from Grandmother and Grandfather's house. Mama said I wouldn't have far to walk to school.

I liked the house we moved into. It had a cement porch on two sides of it where ladybugs had meetings in the sun sometimes. I watched them and wondered if they were all ladies or if there were some gentlemen. I never heard of gentlemen bugs, but there must be some. Mama said every living thing had to have mamas and daddies. I concluded that those ladybugs were having a missionary meeting. The ladies in our church did that and sewed and talked and talked and then ate sandwiches and drank coffee. Sometimes they packed barrels with clothes and stuff to send to the missionaries. I asked Mama what *missionaries* meant, and she said they were people who went to Africa to tell the heathens about Jesus. That was too much for me to think about. I didn't even know what Africa was or what *heathens* meant. I did know a little about Jesus but thought I'd wait until I knew more before I tried to find out why the heathens had to know about Him too.

Once my grandma, that is my mama's mother, had a missionary meeting at her house and a lot of ladies were there. They were packing two barrels to send to the missionaries. Someone talked about the missionary and said he had a little boy and a little girl and those poor children didn't have anything. I really felt bad about a little girl who didn't have anything and, when nobody was looking, I dropped my rag doll which I'd gotten for Christmas in the barrel. My little brother saw me and he dropped his teddy bear in also. We didn't tell Mama about it for several days, but when we did, she cried. I never could figure out why. I didn't think she loved that doll as much as I did. Was it because of Buddy's teddy bear?

15

I laughed when I watched those ladybugs. *Their missionary barrel would surely be small. What would they put in it? I might need Grandma's magnifying glass to see—the ones she used sometimes when she read her Bible. Do ladybugs know about Jesus? Does Jesus care about ladybugs?* It was all very puzzling.

I dreamed about starting to school for so long, I was about to run out of imaginary events. There were two grade schools in Bentley, Kansas. The Lincoln School was in the east end of town and the Washington School in the west end. My aunt and uncle and my two cousins had moved to the west end, and so Barbara Jean would be going to the Washington School. She told my brother and me that she would still play with us but might not see us as often because they were moving to the west end. That is where all the really "uppity-ups" live. The east end wasn't so bad, though. The really bad place was the north end. That was on the other side of the railroad tracks and all the bootleggers lived down there. I had never been there and wasn't too sure what a bootlegger was.

When that wonderful first day finally arrived, Mama walked with me. We left Buddy off at Grandmother's house on the way. We saw other mothers and children also walking. When we got to the schoolyard I didn't want to go in. The gray stone building looked larger than any I had seen before, except for the post office. The school had an upstairs and a downstairs.

Some other children were playing in the yard, swinging on the swings, flying around on some metal rings on chains attached to a pole; or just chasing each other, laughing and having a good time. Their happiness made me unhappy. How could I ever get to know this place the way they did? I had always known only small groups of people, mostly family. Mama said, "The children playing in the schoolyard are from the older grades. When you have gone to school a year, you will know your way around the building and playground the way they do." I wasn't sure, but felt some better.

There wasn't much time to think about what I wanted or didn't want. Mama took me right into the building and up to the first-grade room. Kindergarten was a new thing in our town and it was possible to skip it and go directly into the first grade. When we got into the classroom I felt better and became excited again. The teacher, who sat behind the desk, smiled at us. Other mothers and children were in the room, walking around inspecting the desks, the pictures on the wall and the blackboards.

A mother and little boy had been sitting, talking with the teacher. The teacher excused herself and got up to shake hands with my mother. Mama pushed me in front of her and said, "This is Bonnie May. She has been looking forward to school." The teacher, Miss Brown, had very kind eyes. I thought she was the most beautiful person I had ever seen, except maybe my mother.

"Come, Bonnie May," she held out her hand, "I'll show you where your seat is and you can put your things away."

A desk all my own. That was amazing! I proudly arranged my tablet, my reader, my arithmetic book and my two new pencils. When my parents had bought the school things the week before, I wanted to start using the new red tablet right away. There was a picture on the front of an Indian chief, in his feather hat. I had never owned a tablet all for myself, and I felt very rich when Mama let me put my name on this one. I knew my alphabet and didn't see why I couldn't start filling up the blank pages. Mama said no, they'd be used up soon enough and times were getting hard. We would have to be sure we didn't waste anything. Even tablets and pencils.

My mother didn't stay long and neither did any of the other mothers. One little boy cried and that mother stayed longer than the rest. I wouldn't have let anyone see me cry, even if it killed me. I acted very cheerful. Miss Brown explained to us all about recess and lunch time and how we must all be careful when we walked across streets to go home. She told us that one part of the playground was for children under the fourth grade and the other part for the older grades. We must always stay in our part during school hours. And never, ever go in any other door than the one we went out.

We got out our readers and looked at them. We would be reading the first two pages for the next day. Those first two pages didn't have a story, just the alphabet, some words spelled out and some pictures beside them. Miss Brown said she would be helping us with this the next day and there would be special exercises for those who didn't know their alphabet yet.

Recess was fun. We just explored around our part of the schoolyard and played on things. I liked the merry-go-round most. It was the kind that someone had to push to make it go round. If we all pushed, it would go really fast and then we could jump on quickly and ride free for awhile. There was a teetertotter, and I didn't get on that; but when I saw an empty swing, I jumped on to swing for awhile.

I heard a whistle, but I didn't see Miss Brown. I slid out of the swing and ran around the building to a door. There was a line of older boys and girls getting ready to go in. *Must be the wrong door.* I ran around another corner and saw a door, but there weren't any children there…or teachers. No one. So I turned and ran back, but I couldn't find a door that looked like ours. Soon it was very still on the playground. Everyone was inside and I couldn't find the right door. I was all alone.

I knew I couldn't go in the wrong door. That was against the rules. One thing I knew for sure: I wasn't going to break any rules the first day. Another thing I knew: I knew how to walk home.

And that is what I did.

Well, I didn't walk. I think I ran. I needed to see someone familiar. Mama was surprised when I burst breathlessly into the house. She was dusting a table and stood holding the dustcloth in one hand.

"What are you doing home? Did something happen at school? Are you sick?" She had enough questions, I thought. Why didn't she just hug me and say everything would be all right?

I explained what happened and told her I really liked school but just couldn't find that silly door to go back in after recess. She didn't scold; she simply said, "Well, we'll try again tomorrow."

The telephone rang then, and it was our ring—four shorts and a long. I heard Mama telling the teacher that I was all right and that I would be back the next day. I thought about how I had dreamed and planned so long for the first day of school, and then it turned out to be kind of a short day—a bit disappointing, not anything like my dreams. I was learning that what is real isn't always what you expected it to be. Oh well, maybe tomorrow would be better.

CHAPTER TWO

GATHERING CLOUDS

Constant change seemed to be the norm in our family. For all my growing up time and throughout the depression years, when mobility was not so common as it is today, we were the most mobile family I knew. The reasons were varied.

I recall that first school year, when we were apparently so settled and happy, life was suddenly disrupted again. We moved from our house, with all those lovely ladybugs, into a large house with Grandma and Grandpa Loring.

I overheard Mama and Grandma talking one day about the baby that was about to come. I supposed someone was going to be bringing a baby to see us. I didn't suspect the move had anything to do with that. What I didn't know—

and in those days adults didn't discuss such things with children—was that when my brother was born, the doctor had told my parents there should be no more babies. My mother could not survive another delivery. Now there was to be one and Grandma thought Mama should be with her so she could take care of things. I learned all of this many years later.

Circumstances for Buddy and me weren't too different. We were somewhat spoiled by grandparents and aunts and uncles. I had to share the attention with Buddy but school made up for that. I loved school. I especially loved to read. Mama got a library card for me, and we went to the library and checked out two books once a week. I would walk home very slowly, reading all the way. By the time we reached home, I had read both books and there was a week to reread them. They were very simple books, of course, but I felt caught up in the midst of world affairs because I could read. When Buddy would sit still, I would read to him.

I was very fond of my grandpa. He talked with us as though we were grown-up people. My mama had been his favorite "little girl" I think. It was not easy for me to imagine my mama as a little girl. To me she was Mama who was always there when I needed her. She was almost always happy and seldom worried about tomorrow. I don't think my grandpa liked my Daddy very much and that made me sad.

One day I came home from school and Mama was in bed and I had a new sister. Such a tiny little thing; they called her Dora Lynne. Mama said she was very healthy and they both felt fine. I looked at the baby's tiny little ears. Her eyes were shut tight and I asked Mama what color they were. She said, "All babies' eyes are blue at first. They may change to brown like yours later. Would you like to see her feet?"

She uncovered the baby's feet and I counted ten little pink toes. I touched them. They were soft and warm. She wiggled a little and made a funny little noise with her mouth. I thought, *Babies aren't so bad. This one is pretty quiet and doesn't seem to be much trouble.* I did hope Mama would get out of bed soon though. I didn't like seeing her in bed in the daytime.

As the days went by, the only change for me was that I didn't get to go to the library every week. Mama had to stay inside with Dora Lynne. Grandma took care of both of them and kept the house tidy.

I practiced reading from my first-grade reader and tried to read the words on everything around the house. Grandma had a box of soap called Jumbo Cleanser. It had a picture of a fat, mama elephant in an apron sitting on a three-legged stool. There was a washtub in front of her with a baby elephant sitting in it, having her Saturday night bath. On the floor beside the tub was a box of soap just like ours with a picture of the elephants and their soap box. I thought, *What if I stepped into the picture on our box and into the picture on the box in the picture, and on and on.* It made me dizzy to think about. There didn't seem to be anywhere to end. Mysterious.

One day I overheard my two uncles and Daddy and Mama talking. Uncle Bob was saying, "I got this chance to buy some good land in Missouri. Anything will grow on it. Why don't we go there and farm? There is an old stone house we can all live in until we make enough to build." Daddy and Mama agreed that with jobs getting so scarce it might be a good idea.

Before I had time to ask many questions or dream about what Missouri would be like, we were on our way there. At first, leaving my beloved Miss Brown and first grade was disheartening. But Daddy said I could take my books and keep on studying at home. That made me feel somewhat better. He got me a new Indian chief tablet and a new yellow pencil.

We stayed in Missouri for less than a year, and the next summer we were back in Kansas. We moved into a house in Scandia, which was about fifteen miles from Bentley. Daddy would be working for a farmer, Mama said.

Buddy and I had a great time exploring the new yard. My brother was two years younger than I but much braver. He could climb trees higher, run faster and turn better somersaults. There wasn't anything he wouldn't try, and I spent much of my time following and scolding, "Buddy, be careful....Don't do that....Don't go so far."

He just laughed at me usually and said, "Scaredy cat." He was a skinny little freckle-faced boy with pale blue eyes and sandy hair. Both of us had Buster Brown haircuts—Buddy's just a bit shorter than mine.

About this time Daddy informed us that we should stop calling my brother "Buddy" and call him by his real name: Herbert. Daddy said if he started to school with a nickname like that, he would have it all his life. I didn't see anything wrong with that. I found it rather disturbing to have to change. Changing a name is almost like changing a person, and I liked my brother the way he was; even if I did have to spend a lot of time warning him to be careful. There wasn't any choice, really. Mama agreed with Daddy and what he said we did. So, from then on, Buddy was Herbert.

Our new yard had a big cottonwood tree in it and Daddy put up a tire swing for us. We spent hours in that swing, taking turns pushing each other or sometimes sitting in it and twisting the rope as tightly as we could in one direction. Then we'd lift our feet off the ground and hang onto the tire while it unwound very fast. When we got out we were so dizzy that we would stagger all over the yard. We called it getting drunk.

Neither of us had seen any drunk people, but we had heard about them. We never had alcohol in our house. Grandma said, "Liquor is the devil's tool."

One day, we went to visit Grandma and Grandpa Loring. Mama and Grandma went shopping and left Buddy and me at Grandma's house. Daddy and my uncles were there. Uncle Bob said, "Wait 'til you see what I've got in the cellar."

He left and came back with a jar of something that smelled sort of like Mama's bread dough starter. He said, "This is some of the best peach brandy I ever made and I think it's about ready." He poured out a little glass for each of the men, and Buddy—that is, Herbert—came running up and begged for some. Uncle Bob let him taste from his glass. Herbert licked his lips as though he liked it. Uncle Bob asked if I wanted to taste it and I shook my head "No." I wouldn't want to eat bread dough starter and didn't think I'd like anything that smelled like it.

The men sat around and talked for awhile and every time one of them set his glass down Herbert sneaked another sip. I don't know how much he drank, but when Mama and Grandma came home Herbert was walking like he'd just gotten out of our twisty tire swing.

Grandma scolded Uncle Bob. That was really something to see a grown man get a scolding. He just kind of chuckled under his breath as he took the jar of brandy back to the cellar. I guess he was afraid Grandma would throw it out if he didn't hurry. Grandma was saying something about "the devil's ways..."

I began to wonder about the devil after that. I asked my Sunday school teacher about him and she said, "Oh, he's always at work and he wants us to do bad things." That wasn't very good information so far as I was concerned. *How would I even know him if I saw him? Could he be everywhere? Could I hide from him?* I didn't do such bad things. Even when I got an occasional spanking for not minding Mama, it was because *I* had decided not to mind; not because I heard any devil tell me to be naughty.

Then one day I heard my grandma say in very serious tones, "The devil lives over there in that convent." My grandparents' house was across the street from a Catholic convent. The nuns living there were nurses at Bentley's one hospital. I had seen the "sisters" in their black gowns as they walked on the grounds. They looked harmless enough. They usually smiled at everyone, but the fact that they wore flowing black made the story credible to my childish ears.

So far as I know, this was my first brush with prejudice of any kind. Oh, there were other prejudices in our family. I just hadn't seen them yet. My grandmother, at that time, was certain that no good thing could come out of the Catholic church. When I overheard her and other women from our church describing the Catholics, I shivered for fear I might meet one sometime in the dark.

Not long after Grandma's remark about the residence of the devil, we went to Bentley to do some errands. It was getting late, and Herbert and I went to sleep in the car. I woke with a start and realized that it was dark and we were alone in the car parked in front of Grandma's house—across from the convent. Suddenly I saw something big and black flying in the sky and settling down as if to land on the convent grounds. Whatever it was changed its course and flew straight to the window of our car. I heard: "Now you have seen the devil. Be sure you do not tell your folks about this."

I grabbed Buddy and hung on with all my might. Then the form disappeared. My teeth chattered as I said, "Buddy, are you afraid to run into the house? Shall we tell Mama and Daddy?" He didn't say anything but, by then, was out of the car and halfway to Grandma's front porch. I was close behind him and we were soon inside. Neither of us spoke at first. Everyone must have assumed we were afraid of the dark.

Later, I told Mama about the incident and she said, "Well, you probably dreamed it. You were asleep when we went into the house." I agreed with her because that seemed to be the safest assumption. There was a lingering doubt, however. *What if…?*

The next week, school started and I was very happy to be in first grade again. I had missed too much the year before to go on to the second grade, and Mama said since I hadn't gone to kindergarten I wouldn't actually be behind.

I was the star pupil the first two months because I was merely reviewing what I had already learned. There were new experiences, too. The teacher was different and her methods were not the same as Miss Brown's. I especially liked the memorizing part. My new teacher, Miss Anderson, had us memorize poetry. One of the first poems I memorized was called *September*.

I was captivated with the phrases: "The goldenrod is yellow...." I had seen goldenrod and knew how beautiful it can be in the fall. "The gentian's bluest fringes are curling in the sun...." I didn't know what gentian was, but could imagine a blue flower with curling petals. I enjoyed the musical sound of the words and repeated the phrases over and over.

Daddy worked most of the time, but some of the time he was sick and couldn't work. Mama always smiled and said, "Don't worry. We still have food on the table." Many of the grown up people seemed to be worried about other things. They talked about the troubles in Europe. I didn't know where Europe was but wasn't bothered by that. Mama held our home together with her smile and nothing seemed different except that we didn't have as much meat on the table as when I was very young. I loved vegetables and so didn't even miss the meat. We nearly always had chicken for Sunday dinner.

Mama raised chickens every year. She saved some of the pullets for laying hens, and then we had the others to eat all winter. I never got tired of chicken. I couldn't stand to watch anyone chop their heads off, though. Daddy was the same way. Mama said he was *chicken-hearted*. She would chop off their heads and, when they stopped flopping, Daddy dipped them in boiling water and plucked the feathers off. Mama could cut them up so neatly for frying or sometimes take the insides out and roast the chicken whole. When she roasted a chicken, she put dressing in it. If it was an old hen that had quit laying or an old rooster they had killed, she boiled it until it was tender and then dropped dumplings into the bubbling broth.

Sometimes Mama made egg noodles. We enjoyed watching her make them. She stirred up the yellow dough, rolled it out thin and then cut the narrow noodles. She spread them on the bread board for half a day to dry before putting them into the hot broth for supper. Sometimes she put them outside in the sun and put a cheesecloth over them to keep the flies away. They dried faster then. Usually Herbert and I would get one before it was cooked and chew on it. They weren't very good that way.

That school year I had my first close girlfriend. We walked to and from school together, discussed our private thoughts, and swore each other to secrecy in case either of us did anything wrong. We hated tattletales. Twice, as a team, we almost did get in trouble. Well, once it was almost and the other time I got in trouble.

One day as we were walking home from school we took a shortcut through someone's back yard. My friend, Thelma, said some people she knew lived there, and they wouldn't care if we pulled some of the carrots and vegetables from the garden. "Actually," she bragged, "they said that since I am such a good friend, I can come over here anytime I want and help myself. So you can, too."

We had a fine time pulling plump carrots, mostly just to see how easy it was as they popped out of the ground. Then we decided to pull a few radishes. There were some little, fat red ones and some long white ones. We didn't want to eat them because they are better with salt.

I said, "Thelma, look at all this lettuce. Did you ever pick any for your mother?" She hadn't. It was time for me to display my unusual knowledge. I showed her how to break the large leaves from the outside of the plants. "But we'd better not pick any more because lettuce has to be cleaned right away and kept cool, and we don't have anywhere to do that," I said.

Thelma looked up startled. "What's that? I hear someone coming. Let's get out of here." She ran across the yard and squirmed under a lilac hedge, with me right behind.

"I thought you knew the people," I panted.

"Well, I really just know someone who knows them." She was probably lying about even that, I thought as I ran across the next yard and out onto the brick sidewalk in front. I didn't bother to say goodbye to Thelma. I was home in about two minutes and didn't tell anyone about the incident.

The next day at school Thelma told me she heard the people were real mad and were going to call the police, and we would probably have to go to jail. We could still be friends in jail. I didn't much like the prospect. For about a week I worried a lot but didn't confide in anyone. Every time I left for school, I stayed far from the house with the vegetable garden. I always looked to see if the police were anywhere around. I knew what a policeman's uniform looked like from a picture in one of my books. I had never seen one in Scandia. There was an old building which someone said was the jail. It had bars on the windows and weeds growing in the yard. I never saw anyone go in there.

Eventually I convinced myself that we were not going to be discovered as criminals. But I had learned one lesson: I hoped I would never take anything again that didn't belong to me, and I planned to stay out of other people's yards.

The next time Thelma and I got in trouble was somewhat different. I, at least, did get caught and it was humiliating. This day we had come home from school down our two-block-long Main Street. It was out of our way, but sometimes there are interesting things to see on Main Street. We could look in the store windows and talk about

some of the things we'd like to have. We stopped in front
of Haley's Drug Store. Thelma said if she were rich she
would buy the big bottle of perfume in the window. I said
if I had a million dollars I would buy the dresser set in the
window. There was a brush, a comb and a mirror with a
handle. The back of the brush and mirror were made of
pearl, and there was a pink flower on the comb. I never
saw a comb with a flower on it before.

We walked very slowly and talked about all the things
we'd buy if we had a million dollars. Then we came to the
dry-goods store where the old men sat on a bench in front
of the store—I mean, really old. Seems they must all be
about a hundred. Some of them were chewing tobacco and
spitting out toward the street. You had to be careful when
you walked in front of them.

Just then Thelma got an idea. "See that old man there
with the brown stocking cap?" she asked.

"Yes, why?" She explained that she kind of knew him.
I remembered our experience in some people's garden.

She hurried on to explain, "His name is Joe Jensen
and he always says 'Hi, Thelma' when I go by." She added,
"One time he gave me a penny, and maybe if I ask him he
will give me another and we can get some jelly beans."

I followed her a bit reluctantly. It sounded all right,
and then again it didn't. Too late, she was already saying,
"Hi, Joe."

He said, "Hi, Thelma."

She said, "That was sure nice of you to give me that
penny that time."

He said, "What did you do with it?"

"Spent it."

"'Spose you'd like another one?"

"Well, my friend and I—her name's Bonnie May...."

"Hello, Bonnie May," he shook hands with me and I felt rather silly. No one shook hands with children.

Thelma continued, "Bonnie May was just saying that it would sure be nice if we had some jelly beans to eat on the way home." I didn't like her saying that, but Joe started to laugh. He laughed so hard I thought he might fall off the bench or choke on the tobacco wad. When he quit laughing he dug down in his pocket and got out two pennies.

As he handed us each a penny, he said, "Now, you make those jelly beans last a long time, because there aren't any more where those come from." I felt kind of bad about that but took the penny anyway.

On the way home, we were eating the candies very slowly—one bean a block. I thought I'd save two for Mama. She always shared special treats with me. Mama was getting supper when I got home. She said, "You're a little late, Bonnie May. Did you and Thelma stop somewhere to play after school?"

I said no, but we did come through downtown and a man gave us some money and we bought some candy. I opened my fist and held out a sticky palm, damp from the red and blue jelly beans. "I saved two for you."

Mama didn't even look pleased. In fact, she looked worried and mighty displeased. She didn't take the candy. "Who did you say gave you the pennies?"

"A man named Joe, somebody that Thelma sort of knows."

"Did you girls ask for the money?"

"Well, yes, I guess so."

While I stood there awkwardly holding two sticky jelly beans in my hand, Mama gave me one good scolding. At first, I wasn't sure what we had done that was so wrong. By the time Mama was through talking, I knew that good children never ask for money; that girls, especially little girls, never take a present from men; and that it is best not to speak to someone you do not know unless your parents are with you. I didn't know why all this was true, but I knew Mama and she had never been wrong; so I didn't have to know why. I was so embarrassed that I stood there wishing she would spank me instead of talking to me. But that was another thing: Mama knew when to spank and when to talk.

Finally, she said firmly, "Now, throw those jelly beans away and wash your hands for supper. We won't say any more about it." And we never did.

At the end of the school year, we moved again; this time to Murray, Kansas. Murray was only a little larger than Scandia. So far as Daddy was concerned, the first matter of business after we got our furniture all moved in and the beds set up was to make sure of a storm shelter. When a place didn't have a storm cellar, Daddy dug one. He knew a great deal about tornadoes and about storm caves. He knew just how deep to dig, how to reinforce the sides and roof with heavy beams, and he always finished the outside into a hard-packed mound that looked as though a giant elephant were buried there. We children had a game we played on the mound. We called it King of the Mountain.

We were soon all helping Daddy haul dirt in wheelbarrows, buckets and baskets. Mama didn't help much. Storms didn't worry her, and she didn't think it was worth the effort of digging your own cave; but she didn't mind if Daddy went ahead with it because he felt it was so necessary to protect his family. When the job was all done, we children thought it was exciting to fix up the cave. Daddy put some old, canvas army cots down there and a table with kerosene lamps on it. He made some shelves so Mama could keep her jars of canned vegetables and fruit down where it was cool.

One evening some friends came over to visit and the grownups were sitting out in the yard visiting. It was still light. The day had been very hot and humid. Sometimes a Kansas day is quite sweaty. Those are the humid days. Those are also the days that someone says, "A storm is brewing." Other times, the day is dry, dusty and windy. I liked those days best because I didn't like to sweat and I didn't like storms.

On this particular evening, we children were playing King of the Mountain on the cellar mound. Our friend, Cleo, was king. Herbert and I and Cleo's little brother all got caught trying to sneak over the mound, so we were slaves of Cleo. We followed her around in a follow-the-leader game where we had to do everything she did. We walked like frogs, did somersaults, stood on our heads and ran as fast as we could three times around the house. Then we all dropped laughing and exhausted in the dirt.

In the distance, we heard a rumble of thunder and all of us sat up to look for the lightning. Cleo's dad said, "Those are mean-looking clouds. We'll have to go home soon, or maybe we'll just stay and try out your new storm cellar." We children, of course, were hoping they would.

We watched the clouds. The sun was just going down and we could see a ragged rim of clouds in the northwest. They were black and gray and rolling. Suddenly, someone said "Look at that tornado!" Along the ragged rim, a little half circle had formed and dropped away from the mass of clouds. It writhed, rolled and moved by itself—dipping and rising. By this time it had a twisty tail on it. Daddy said it was so far away that it wouldn't reach us because it was traveling around us. "But we'd better keep an eye on it anyway. They're sneaky things, and there may be others."

Mama told us children to stay close by the house and not to run around any more for awhile. We were glad to do just as she said. Cleo was two years older than I and a natural leader. She also had a very good imagination. She told us that there was a magic way of protecting ourselves. "Here's what you do," she said. "You dig a little pretend cave and fix it up all nice as if a tiny fairy would be getting in it. If you get it done before the storm hits, you won't be hurt."

So we four did as Cleo instructed and our time was occupied until the storm clouds had broken up and there was no more danger of a storm, for now. Then it was time to go inside and have some refreshments before our friends went home.

On another day when we were out playing with Cleo, we were walking down the middle of a side street that went along one side of our house. We looked up and saw a large hawk hovering just above us. Herbert said, "I heard they can pick up children."

Cleo never missed an advantage. "Oh, they can," she replied. "In fact, there is only one thing to do when one goes over. Drop down flat where you are as soon as you see it."

So Herbert and I dropped down in the middle of the dusty street. We asked Cleo how we'd know when the hawk was gone, and she said she would let us know. We heard Mama calling, "Bonnie May, Herbert, what are you doing in the middle of the street?" We looked up rather sheepishly and said there was a hawk. Cleo was standing there laughing and were we mad! Mama said, "Well, get up right now before you get run over." We never told her that Cleo was to blame, though she probably knew. Tattling was almost as bad as lying, to us children.

Those were the beginnings of the depression days, and I heard people talking about hard times. We children didn't worry much about hard times. Our lives were full. Mama and Daddy loved each other and all of us. There was always something to do, and we didn't even know that some people might have more possessions than we had. It wasn't important.

Daddy did not always have a job. He had been wounded in the war—something they called *shell shock*. He got a very small pension which was enough to pay our rent. He was sick much of the time; but when he was well, he either worked for someone or helped my grandfather in his truck garden. We always had fresh vegetables, and Mama canned fruit in the fall. Our folks managed to buy a bushel or two of apples and pears to can. Some of the apples were put into the cellar to eat fresh all winter.

When Daddy was sick, I worried. He would turn pale and have chills. Even in the summer time. Mama piled quilts and blankets on him and fixed a hot water bottle or hot bricks wrapped in an old towel. I thought it must have been a terrible war to cause my daddy to get so sick.

CHAPTER THREE

WHERE DID
HE COME FROM?

The next few years must have been difficult ones for my parents. Daddy was sick as much as he was well. There seemed to always be a new baby in the house. We didn't actually go hungry, but sometimes we didn't know where the next sack of flour was coming from; and that was vitally important. We needed to be able to count on making bread. Sometimes that was all we had to eat.

Mama taught me at a very early age how to mix and knead bread. She had a *starter* in a large jar. Once a week, or sometimes twice, we would get out the large, tin dishpan. We had only one pan large enough to mix so much bread. Mama was scrupulously clean. After each dishwashing, the pan had to be scoured, rinsed with cold water and scalded with hot water from the teakettle. Before we mixed the bread, the dishpan was cleaned again. I have always had an extremely sensitive sense of taste for anything not right in food, and I do not remember ever noticing the taste of soap in our bread. I *do* remember our family visiting some friends several times for fried chicken dinners, and I always thought I tasted soap on the chicken. As much as I loved fried chicken, I didn't like going there to eat.

After we had the pan ready, we put in milk and shortening (usually lard) and heated this on the back of the woodburning range. Then in a crock we made a *sponge* from a portion of the starter, adding some sugar, flour and water. This was covered with a clean cloth and set in the sun to rise.

In about an hour the sponge had risen to the top of the crock and the bread dough could be mixed. We put the sponge, some salt, more sugar and more flour in the dishpan of warm milk and lard. Then the whole thing had to be mixed and dumped on a floured breadboard to knead into a smooth dough. We would clean and grease the dishpan and put the dough back in it, cover it with a clean tea towel, and set it in the sun. This dough-rising usually took about an hour also; and then more kneading and shaping of the loaves. There would be about ten loaves of bread, some dinner rolls, and sometimes (if we had the ingredients) some cinnamon rolls. When the loaves had risen double, it was time to put them in the oven.

I learned how to make these large amounts of bread at an age when most girls were still jumping rope or playing with dolls. I knew every aspect of the breadmaking just as

Mama did, but I couldn't have written out a recipe. Mama didn't have one and neither would I.

Ah, the fragrance of fresh baked bread! We always got to eat a crust while it was still hot, spread with butter that melted right away. If we didn't have butter, we didn't mind; anything on it was good—or nothing at all. Herbert liked his with a little sugar sprinkled on it. I didn't care much for the taste of sugar.

I think that because we got so much enjoyment from the simple things, we didn't miss what we couldn't have. Coming in from school with the house full of the aroma of fresh baked bread, the clean fragrance of a freshly scrubbed kitchen floor or clothes just taken from the line, made me glad to be alive. Always having Mama there smiling helped.

When I assisted with the breadmaking and used the last of the flour, which Daddy brought home in 100-pound sacks, I became worried; especially when Daddy was sick and I knew there wasn't money to buy any more. But Mama had a quality I didn't have. She lived for today and enjoyed each day. She would answer my worries with, "Don't borrow tomorrow's troubles. We are eating today." Then she would add one of her favorite quotations from the Bible, "Take no thought for tomorrow...tomorrow will take care of itself. Sufficient unto the day is its own evil." I think she paraphrased it for my benefit. She had taught us that, if the Bible says so, it is so; and I believed her. I still worried some.

Another worry I had was about the number of babies we had. By the time I was in the fifth grade there were seven of us. I was naive. My parents didn't talk about having babies. They just had them. I had quite a collection of wrong ideas about where babies originated. I remember that during my second year of school I had questioned Mama many times. She either did not know how or what to tell me, or she did not think children should be told such things. At any rate, she always answered, "You are too young. You would not understand. When you are older, you will know."

I finally exhausted every source I knew of and gave up the quest. I decided that the doctor who came to our house each time a baby was born brought the baby in his little black bag. I also decided that every time Daddy grew a mustache we had a new baby. There had to be some connection. Further than this, I put the whole thing in the back of my mind for several years.

I enjoyed the new babies because, as the oldest in the family, I was allowed to hold them first, carry them around and generally play they were my family. It was better than having dolls. Dolls became very scarce around our house except the homemade, stuffed kind. When this real, live doll had any kind of problem, I could give it back to Mama.

When Daniel James was born, as usual I had not known he was about to be. It was Friday, February 13, and we had our valentine exchange at school. This was a great highlight of the year. For weeks a committee, chosen by drawing names out of a hat, had worked on making a beautiful valentine box. It was covered with red paper and had large, lacy hearts pasted on its sides. The top had a big slot to put the valentines in. For a week before the big day, we were allowed to bring our valentines and push them through the slot.

Everyone made their own valentines. This entailed much planning and collecting of various colors of paper and bits of lace, ribbon and pretty pictures. The artwork was one thing, but deciding who should get them was quite another. We had drawn names and had to give to the person whose name we drew. Then a person's best friend got the prettiest. We usually gave the teacher one. Important decisions had to be made as to the rest of our list, those we wanted to include or leave out. If there was a boy you liked very much, you could get someone to write the name on the envelope of a beautiful valentine card; but you never, never, never signed your name on it. That was part of the mystery; part of the fun. The excitement built up as we saw our friends slip valentines into the box and as we slipped in our own carefully constructed valentines.

I came home from school that day eager to show off my collection of valentines. The teacher had given one to each of us, and I had enough others to make me very happy. There was even a no-name one. I hoped it wasn't from that old Johnny Davis. I couldn't stand him. I hoped it was from Delbert Wilson. I was in love with him.

As I walked into the house I was surprised to see that a neighbor lady we called Grandma Simpson was there. "Where's Mama?" I asked. She nodded toward the bedroom. I took my precious stack of valentines with me, and was surprised to see Mama in bed. "Are you sick, Mama?"

"Not very," she answered with a smile. She did look kind of pale, though. "Let's see your valentines," she suggested and I spread them all out on the bed to show her.

When she had finished examining them, she said, "That is really nice. Now I have a valentine to show you." She lifted the covers behind her and there was another tiny baby. Somehow, I just couldn't appreciate this one. There were too many already, I thought.

That evening we had a program at school and our class was performing. After supper, I got into my heart costume and Daddy took Herbert and me to school. We met in our classroom, and the teacher gave us all a warning to pay attention when she was leading our song tonight and not to giggle the way we did at practice. We lined up on the stairs behind the stage to wait our turn. Johnny Davis was right in front of me. He turned around and grinned. I never did like him. He was mean and had very bad manners.

He said, "Hear you got another baby."

I thought I might as well be rude also. "What's it to you?"

He laughed and said loudly, "Hey, everybody, know what Bonnie May has? Another *ba-a-a-by*." He dragged out the words. Then, when he had everyone's attention, he added, "Those Johnsons, seven come eleven." I didn't know what he meant by that, but some of the boys laughed and repeated, "Seven come eleven."

I was glad when the program was over and Daddy came to pick Herbert and me up. Later, when I got him alone, I asked Herbert what Johnny meant when he said, "Those Johnsons, seven come eleven."

Herbert, in a rather superior tone, said, "Bonnie May, you are so dumb. This baby is the seventh. 'Seven come eleven' is something people say when they are shooting dice. He meant there would probably be eleven Johnson kids." Shooting dice was gambling, I knew. But that was all I knew about it. I wondered how Herbert knew so much.

The next week, my friend Annie Jones asked me if I'd like to go home at noon with her to eat. I asked Mama and she said I could. Annie was two years older than I, but we often walked to school together because she lived on the next block over from us.

When we got to Annie's house, there was no one at home. Her mother had left a note saying that there was a pot of beans on the stove and to help ourselves. It seemed strange to me to go into an empty house like that. There was always someone at our house when we came home.

Anyway, we sat eating the beans and talking. I told Annie about the baby that we called Danny. I had gotten over my first disappointment and was beginning to like him. I also told her about Johnny and how he had embarrassed me in front of everyone. I hoped there wouldn't be eleven of us. Seven seemed like quite a lot when Daddy didn't even have a job. I liked to talk and Annie was a good listener. I said I guessed it wasn't anybody's fault if there were so many babies.

When I said that she looked at me strangely. "Bonnie May, do you know where babies come from?" she asked.

I shook my head. "Well, I haven't thought much about it for a long time, but I think they are brought by the doctor in his black bag." Annie was a very kind friend and didn't even smile at that.

She said, "Bonnie May, you sure have a lot to learn and I don't intend to be your teacher. But I will tell you this: Babies don't come in black bags. They come out of your mother's stomach."

I became very quiet and didn't do any more talking. We went back to school and I pondered Annie's educational remark for a long time.

There was an incident the summer before on the farm. Grandpa Loring and family had moved to a farm. Herbert and I and my cousin Billy were visiting. Herbert and Billy were out at the barn with Grandpa. They asked him why the mare didn't have a colt. He said she hadn't been bred. They ran into the house and asked Grandma for a loaf of bread. They told her Grandpa wanted it so that the mare could have a colt. Everyone, the adults that is, seemed to think that was pretty funny. There must have been some kind of connection, but I just couldn't put it all together. I gave up trying to figure it all out. The black bag theory had served me well enough up to now. I wasn't going to grapple with a new theory—one I didn't understand. Not just yet, anyway.

The next summer was an unusually hot one. The house we lived in was situated next to an open field on one side. The owner had planted the field in clover this year. The summer breezes blowing across that field of clover made the air several degrees cooler than elsewhere, and the fragrance was free. I loved to toss a blanket on the grass in our front yard and dream my daydreams while enjoying the breeze. Sometimes all the children would join me on the blanket. That always made them think about a picnic.

"Bonnie May, ask Mama if we can have our dinner out here for a picnic." Sometimes she would let us eat there. At other times the children wanted me to read to them as they sprawled all over the blanket, some of them even out in the grass.

I think Mama enjoyed having the house quiet for a while and, as for me, I would rather take the responsibility for brothers and sisters than to do any housework. I was developing a real aversion to any kind of manual labor.

One Fourth of July, we had been allowed to eat our supper on the blanket. When we had cleared all the supper things, Mama said she had a surprise for us. She brought out two boxes of sparklers. Fireworks were unknown in our family in those days when we had trouble finding enough pennies to buy a pound of lard. We thought this was our lucky day! I sent Herbert into the house to get a box of kitchen matches. Mama gave us some specific instructions. "Now you be very careful with those matches. Only Herbert and Bonnie May can light them. And all of you watch the baby." We had Danny on the blanket with us. Mama went back into the house.

On the Fourth of July Daddy usually disappeared. I don't know where he went, but I know he couldn't bear to hear the sound of fireworks; especially the large, loud firecrackers—something to do with the war, I think.

Herbert and I took turns lighting the sparklers and handing them to the others. We started with the oldest and worked down because Jimmy Lee, the next to youngest, was afraid at first. I think he wished he were old enough. Dora Lynne held hers while Herbert lit it, and then she ran all over the front yard pretending she was some kind of fairy waving her magic wand. Edna June was next. She thought she would try throwing hers up in the air and watch it come down. I told her to go to the far corner of the yard if she did that.

Then Allan Dale got his and he found a quiet corner of the porch and just sat there holding his and watching it sparkle. He was our quiet brother. He didn't talk much, but he seemed to do a lot of thinking.

Jimmy Lee wasn't afraid by the time he had seen a few of the sparklers in action. I explained to him that one end was hot and how to hold it so as not to get burned. He was pretty smart for two years old, but he couldn't stay still very long. Every day we had to organize a family search party to find where he had wandered off. Tonight he wasn't wandering. He took his sparkler and tried to imitate Dora Lynne and Edna June. I told him not to throw his up in the air and told Edna June to do something else.

Then Herbert and I took our turns and lit ours. Everyone got three sparklers each with three left over. Herbert and I decided that we'd light those as our pay for doing all the work.

The second time around for everyone, Allan Dale was standing waiting for someone to light his sparkler. We were lighting each sparkler now with the already-lit ones, so I had Edna June hold hers out to light Allan's. They were directly over the open box of matches. A spark must have dropped in the box because suddenly a flame shot up and the whole box was on fire. The children scattered, I snatched up Danny and ran into the house shouting "Mama, Daddy!" Mama, calm as ever, looked the situation over and said there didn't seem to be any harm done. She commended Herbert and me for our quick thinking— Herbert for smothering out the fire with the blanket, and I for picking up the baby first.

The excitement was over and there were still a few more sparklers. Jimmy Lee was jumping up and down holding his second one, still unlit. He was saying, "Light it, light it!" So Mama told us to sit on the porch and finish the sparklers. As I sat there on the top step idly twirling a sparkler, I looked at all those children who were quieter now, studying their lighted sparklers. Where had they all come from?

Jimmy Lee was a constant embarrassment to me that year. He was cute as could be with large brown eyes and a mischievous grin. He had a will stronger than all the rest of us put together. He couldn't get along all afternoon without a nap, and yet we couldn't get him into bed to take it. He played outside with the rest of the children and eventually dropped somewhere to take a nap. It didn't matter where. He could sleep anywhere if he wanted to, and once he went to sleep there was no waking him until the nap was finished.

One day we found him in some tall grass in our driveway just a short while before Daddy would be driving in. Another time we found him curled up in some weeds behind a neighbor's car. Our searching party discovered him as the neighbor came out of the house to get in his car to back out. Jimmy was like a cat with nine lives.

One day our search was useless and all of us were getting worried—even Mama. Daddy had gone to town to the hardware store. Mama called him there and told him that we couldn't find Jimmy Lee anywhere. Maybe he had gone to town with Daddy? Daddy said no, but promised to come home right away and help us look. He went back to the car—it was one of those old touring cars with a running board that had a railing on it— and there he found Jimmy, sound asleep and curled up on the running board. He had ridden downtown that way and hadn't awakened.

Mama and Daddy were lavish with their love for us children. That is probably why we never realized how poor we were. They were also firm and believed in spanking when the occasion warranted. Usually, the spanking was with a sharp switch. I do not remember ever seeing my father take off his belt to spank one of us. I do remember a few times when the boys were almost too old for spankings that he used his razor strap. At any rate, Jimmy had his share of firm treatment, but his response to a spanking was a determination to do again the very thing he had been spanked for. It was apparent that the only way to train him would be to outsmart him.

Toilet training took longer with him than with any of the other children. This was mostly because he didn't like sitting still for more than half a minute. The little potty chair that Mama had used with all the children was just too boring for him. We would unpin his diaper and put him on the chair. The next thing we knew he was running around the house with a naked bottom half and carrying the little potty.

I don't know how long the struggle continued, but finally one day he decided on his own that he did not want to wear diapers any longer. Mama said, "All right, but you will have to go to the toilet like your big brothers." She took him to our outside one-holer and helped him learn how to sit on the hole without falling in. There was a little box there for climbing up and he liked that. The training period was over. Jimmy Lee liked his status of being a "big boy" so much that, when we lost him, we could often find him sitting out there like the big boys. We were glad he never went to sleep out there.

But the next event was also embarrassing to me and to Mama. In the summer, he wore only little short pants. One day a visitor drove up to the front of our house and came to the door. Mama stood at the front screen door talking to the gentleman who wanted to talk to Daddy about some work. Just then, Jimmy came running around the house "naked as a jay bird," as Mama later told Daddy. Mama grabbed Jimmy and took him in the house so fast I wondered what the man might do. I think he waited there until she returned.

Anyway, she pinned a diaper on Jimmy and said, "If you want to act like a baby, then you might as well look like one." He grew up pretty fast after that, and didn't go around without his clothes any more. Mama said, "We may be poor, and there may be a lot of us, but we are going to be respectable."

As the summer had been hotter than usual, the following winter was colder than most. The snow came early that year and stayed late. We children were always glad to see the first snowfall. That was a time for rejoicing. Waking one morning and looking out, we saw that all the world was white. The first snowfall was not often very heavy and did not stay long on the ground. *We must get out in it as soon as possible and make a snowman if there is enough snow.* Sometimes we could find a large smooth area to walk off "fox and geese" tracks. That was a game we played on the tracks which were made to look like a wheel. Everyone had to stay in the track and would be out of the game if he stepped onto the snow. We started at the outside rim and tried to work our way into the center hub. The one who was "it" tried to catch the others as they made their way around the wheel and across the spokes.

The first snow-melting left everything rather ugly and slushy. We would walk around in the mud and wish for another snow. When we had been fortunate enough to roll up enough snow to make a snowman, he melted the first day, and we felt very sad as we looked at the dirty pile of slush where he had stood so proudly.

This winter, the period between snows was very short. By mid-winter, it seemed we had been living in a snow-covered world for a long, long time. Even we children got tired of our snow games and especially tired of walking to school through drifts.

One day it was snowing when I started to school. I was going alone that day because all the other children were getting over colds and Mama thought they shouldn't go out. Going to school while it was snowing wasn't too bad. I liked the feel of the light flakes as they rested on my face. They drifted ever so lightly and settled on my eyelashes. I would stick out my tongue and one would rest on it. I couldn't even taste it. It disappeared so fast. Snowflakes are so beautiful, but so fragile.

The teacher told us that no two snowflakes were exactly alike. *Isn't that amazing?* We often had fun making paper snowflakes by folding the paper many times and then cutting out little bits of it, ending with a snowflake.

After school, I was in a hurry to get home. I slipped into my sweater, coat and stocking cap. My mittens were tied on a long string threaded through the arms of my coat so that I didn't lose them. Lost mittens were a real problem at our house. When I put on my galoshes, I didn't even bother to hook them up. They came up to my knees and had metal clasps that were supposed to be fastened, but that took too long. I slid my homework under my coat so it wouldn't get wet and hurried out the door.

It was still snowing. The walk home was only three blocks, but that first block was a long one. The drifts were higher than they were that morning. Sometimes I would stir up the new, fine snow as I slowly plodded through the drifts. Sometimes I would sink to my knees. That would have been fun if I had taken the time to fasten my galoshes.

Soon the insides of the galoshes were full of snow. It packed very tightly around my legs and ankles. At first, my long underwear and stockings protected me, but soon everything was wet and cold. My legs felt numb. Just when I wondered how I would make the next two blocks home, I heard a friendly voice, "Why Bonnie May, looks like you could use some help."

I was so glad to see Mr. Andrews, a neighbor, and was more grateful after he hoisted me up on his broad and powerful shoulder to carry me the rest of the way home.

I was somewhat of a hero when I got home, except that Mama said she couldn't understand why I didn't buckle my overshoes. She fixed a nice pan of water and had me soak my feet in it. I hadn't been exposed long enough to have even a mild case of frostbite. I was glad of that because I had heard that your toes can fall off with frostbite. Mr. Andrews was certainly my hero that day.

By the first of March, Groundhog Day had come and gone. The groundhog had not seen his shadow so everyone said we would have an early spring. It wasn't so, however, and I quit putting my trust in groundhogs. *What could they know, anyway?* We had another heavy blizzard the first week of March. None of the children went to school that week because the drifts were too high.

One night, after all of us children were in bed, I heard Mama and Daddy talking rather loudly. Mama said, "Go get Mrs. Simpson, and call the doctor." I knew enough by this time to realize we were about to welcome Johnson number eight and I felt a little troubled. I heard the back door slam as Daddy left for Mrs. Simpson's house. She lived behind us on the other street.

Daddy returned in a few minutes reporting, "She will be here as soon as she can get into some clothes. The doctor will come if he can get his car out. Not many of the streets are clear." Then the door to Mama and Daddy's bedroom was closed and I didn't hear anything more for awhile.

The next sound I heard was a new baby's wail.

Mrs. Simpson arrived at the back door and the doctor at the front about the same time. I lay there in the dark thinking about babies. *Well, what do you know! Annie was right. Babies don't come in black bags.* In a way, I was glad to clear out all those cobwebby misconceptions; and, for some reason, I didn't hate Johnny Davis any more. What did it matter if Mama and Daddy had eight of us? They always seemed to have enough love for everyone.

CHAPTER FOUR

WHERE DID HE GO?

When I became really aware of life and its beginnings I also began thinking about death. The questions concerning death were more difficult, and answers from adults were not very helpful.

I remember when I was still in first grade in Bentley. While walking home from school one day, I looked up to see a gas balloon. My parents had talked the night before about this balloon and said a man was going to jump out of it with a parachute. Balloons and parachutes were rare in those days and I realized that I was going to see an exciting event which I hadn't thought about till now.

The balloon was off to my right; that would be north of town a few miles. Then I saw the figure of a man, so small it could be one of my dolls, come away from the balloon, and soon a billowy parachute opened and he was floating there in the sky. That was truly amazing!

Then a strange thing happened. The balloon, like a monster, changed its course—turned and started toward the man. It was also flattening—changing shape. I don't know if the man even saw the balloon coming toward him; but suddenly it was over him and then just seemed to swallow him, and the whole black blob dropped out of sight.

I was troubled because I didn't understand what I had seen, but I knew it had to be bad. When I came into the house, a neighbor was there talking with Mama and Daddy. He said, "Nope, the poor man didn't have a chance. The wind changed too fast."

Daddy just looked grim as he agreed, "Yes, Kansas winds can do that."

It was hard for me to realize what they were saying because I hadn't known any person who died, just small animals—mostly birds. I always felt sorry when I saw a dead bird, though I couldn't say why. It seemed strange to me that a man I had seen alive one minute could be dead the next. I didn't brood about this incident for long because his death hadn't come close enough to touch my life.

A few years later, however, I was confronted with death in a more real way. The first year we lived in Murray, I met a boy whose parents knew my parents. His name was Thomas Robert, and of course we called him Tommy Bob. Our families visited together and I considered Tommy Bob one of my best friends. When his mama cat had kittens, he let me have first choice. I chose an all black one with just a little white diamond on its neck. I named it Tarbaby. In time, Tarbaby became a big, fluffy mama cat herself.

The next winter after Tommy Bob gave Tarbaby to me was the bad snow winter. It was also a bad winter in another way: Many of the boys and girls we knew became sick with a disease called infantile paralysis. Mama said it was very serious and we must pray for all of them. I think Mama must have prayed that none of her children would get it because none of us did. But every time one of us had a cold or complained about hurting anywhere, Mama would feel our forehead for fever and make us stay in out of the cold.

One day Mama said that Tommy Bob had infantile paralysis, which some people called polio. I was worried and sat for a long time holding Tarbaby and doing some praying on my own. I had seen some of the children after they had the disease and they were nearly always crippled. One leg would be smaller than the other, and they usually had to wear braces or use crutches. Some couldn't walk at all. Tommy Bob wouldn't like that. He enjoyed running and playing so much. So my prayers were, "Please, God, don't let Tommy Bob be crippled."

When Mama said, "Bonnie May, I have something to tell you," I knew it was something I didn't want to hear. She put her arm around me and said, "Tommy Bob died this morning."

I had this funny thing about crying in front of anyone, even Mama. Maybe it was because Mama was so careful not to cry in front of us children. So, with my heart about to burst, I broke away from Mama and ran out into the back yard. I crawled under a big lilac bush at the back of our yard and cried until there were no more sobs left in me. I felt dry and dead myself, but I was glad I had cried. Then I sat there for a long time trying to think. *Would I ever see Tommy Bob again? Where did he go? Why did he die?*

I didn't blame God. I was sure my friend must be with Him. Did God like him as much as I did? I just hoped He would let Tommy Bob run and play up there.

Just then Tarbaby found me under the lilac bush and climbed into my lap to be stroked. I rubbed her black, shiny fur and she purred loudly. All I could say then was, "Thank you, Tommy Bob, for Tarbaby." I couldn't remember if I had ever thanked him.

I thought life was going to be very sad without Tommy Bob. So for a few days I didn't even try to smile about anything. Actually, I tried not to smile because I thought that was more loyal. Mama and Daddy were especially kind to me. I expect they had instructed the other children to be kind also, because no one teased or troubled me for several days.

A carnival came to town and somehow Daddy was able to give each of us older children a dime to spend. We could ride on one of the rides for a nickel and buy something to eat with the other nickel. It was the most exciting event of the year and many of our schoolmates were there. I saw the twins, Barbara and Brenda, who were friends from school. We three walked up and down looking at all the rides and all the sideshows.

Barbara said she would like to go into the freak shows, but Brenda reminded her that their mother told them specifically not to go into those. I was curious, but it didn't matter. I knew I didn't have enough money to do that and go on a ride. I would have enough trouble deciding which ride. There was the Ferris wheel. I'd never been on one, but high places kind of scared me, so I didn't think I would choose that. There was a ride that had swings that went way out over the crowd. There was a twisty ride where you got into a car and the car twisted all over, giving your neck a good jerk ever so often. Of course, there was the merry-go-round with the horses—mostly, that was for the younger children.

Walking around was as much fun as anything. There were some funny, wiggly mirrors that you looked into and they either made you too fat or too thin. Either way, you didn't look like yourself.

As we passed the sideshows some of them had platforms in front where a man was trying to get everyone to come in and see his show. On one of them sat the fattest woman I had ever seen. Beside her sat the skinniest man I had ever seen. It made me think of a song that Daddy sometimes sang to us in the evenings. It went something like:

> The thinnest man I ever saw
> Lived down in Hoboken,
> And if you've never seen him
> You'd surely think I'm jokin'.

> He wouldn't go out on a very dark night,
> He wouldn't go out alone,
> For fear some dog'd come along
> And take him for a bone.

There was another verse about someone spitting tobacco juice on him because he looked like a crack in the wall. We children would double up in laughter every time

Daddy came to the last lines. *I must remember to tell him that I saw his man from Hoboken.*

After we had walked and talked and waved at many of our friends, Barbara and Brenda decided to go on the Ferris wheel. I went with them. After all, it was pretty silly to be afraid of high places; especially of a Ferris wheel that doesn't really go anywhere.

It was exciting as we got up high over the carnival grounds and could look out over our little town. We could see our school and the Methodist church and the Congregational church and the Catholic church. There was Main Street and I thought I could see our house, except some trees got in the way. I concluded there wasn't anything to be afraid of. We stopped on the top so they could put someone on at the bottom. Barbara rocked the seat and that frightened me. I tried not to act afraid, but got a little mad instead. I said, "Now, stop that, Barbara Ann. It's dumb to rock these seats because we can't see so well."

Brenda warned, "Well it scares me and I'm going to tell Mama if you don't stop right now."

Barbara gave in but grumbled, "Oh, all right. A couple of babies." I didn't care what she called me so long as she stopped rocking that seat while we were on top. The wheel started going again. Once more around and our ride was over.

After we got off the Ferris wheel we walked around again to see if any more of our friends had arrived since we started our ride. We saw my new neighbor, Darryl. He had moved in across the street from us. He was from California and that made him some kind of a celebrity. I felt important just having him for a neighbor. I told Barbara he had kissed me once, but she didn't believe it. She said he had practically promised to be her boyfriend.

Herbert spent the whole time with five or six of his friends from school. He always ignored me completely when we were out like that. I had left Dora Lynne and Edna June to entertain themselves as they walked around and decided how to spend their money. They found some of their classmates to ride on the merry-go-round with them. Edna June wanted to ride the Ferris wheel, but the others didn't want to.

When it was time to go home, all of us Johnsons gathered at the gate and walked home together. Herbert dragged a little behind us because he was embarrassed to be seen with his sisters. Mama had told us to walk home together because it would be getting dark when we started home. We talked all the way home about the things we had seen and done. Even Herbert joined the conversation as soon as we had gone half a block.

When we got home everything was talked over again for Mama and Daddy. Mama had saved some supper, but we weren't hungry so she didn't insist that we eat.

That night, after I went to bed, I lay for a long time thinking about all we had done. Finally, I realized that I was about to drop off to sleep and should say my prayers. Feeling a bit guilty, I remembered that I had not thought about Tommy Bob all day. I said, "Our Father, which art in heaven, bless Mama and Daddy and all of us and be good to Tommy Bob, please. Amen." I was soon fast asleep.

After a few weeks, I tried to remember what Tommy Bob had looked like. I couldn't remember. I wondered if it were wrong not to be able to remember. I still had Tarbaby and she had kittens. Mama said I didn't have to give all of them away, but could keep the one I liked best. I kept a black one who looked exactly like another little, tiny Tarbaby.

I enjoyed having a cat for a pet, but the boys in our family said they didn't like cats and would rather have a dog. That spring, a stray dog came to our house. Mama didn't see how we could feed it, but she gave in and let the boys keep it anyway. It was a dirty, yellowish mutt. The boys set a washtub of water in the sun to get it warm and then they gave him a bath. He turned out to be pure white and not scrawny at all. He must have come in off a farm where he had been eating rather well.

I hadn't liked dogs much until we got this one. I recalled that when I was in the first grade, while walking home from school one day, a dog had chased me for two blocks until its owner came out and called it back. I was terrified, though the dog probably meant no harm. To me, after that, all dogs were vicious. This dog, however, soon won my affection. No one could decide on a name for him, so we called him Pup. He was about half grown and his puppy heart took in all of us. We became his family and he loved us. The boys would romp in the grass and Pup was always in the middle of the play.

When any of us came outside, he came up and licked us as though he were saying, "I like you particularly." All of us claimed Pup as ours, but the boys said he was especially theirs because I had cats.

There came a time when Pup wasn't interested in the boys' play or anything else that went on around him. He just lay still and wouldn't eat. He even acted a bit unfriendly if we went up to him. Daddy seemed concerned about the whole thing and watched Pup very closely for a couple of days. On a rainy day when we all had to be inside and Pup was under the back porch, I stood watching the raindrops on the window pane. I liked to see the little rivulets chasing each other down the glass. Looking beyond the window I was startled to see Pup had come out from under the porch and was running wildly around the backyard. Herbert joined me at the window and I pointed toward Pup. "What do you think is wrong?"

Just then, Daddy came into the room and looked out the window. He said, "Don't any of you children go outside this house. Do you understand?" We nodded. I looked out the window again. Pup had foam all over his mouth.

Daddy left the room and in a short while we heard the back door slam. Mama was folding clothes on the big dining-room table. "All of you come help me." We gathered around the table and started folding something, anything, awkwardly. My heart was so full of fear that my hands felt numb.

Next we heard a gun shot. All of us jumped, even Mama. She looked at us and said, "Don't stop folding. I'll be right back." She ran to the back door and shouted, "Are you all right?"

We heard Daddy say, "Yes, but keep the children in the house for awhile."

Before very long, Daddy came back in the house, put the rifle on the rack over the door and hung his coat on the hook by the back door. He knew he had to give us some kind of an explanation, but it seemed as hard for him to talk about as the war he had been in. He had always told us only funny or interesting incidents about the war, but never anything very serious.

He said, "I'm sorry, but I had to kill Pup. There was no other way. He would have been dead in a little while anyway, and this way no one else got hurt." That wasn't quite true. We all got hurt, even Daddy. But I knew what he meant. We had heard stories about *mad dogs* and what happened to people who were bit by them.

What I really pondered for a long time was this side of Daddy which I hadn't seen before. He was so soft-spoken and gentle. He couldn't bear to kill a chicken but had killed Pup that he loved even as we all did. I finally asked him, "Daddy, how could you bear to kill the dog and bury him?"

His answer was short, "Some things a man has to do."

I said, "Was it like that in the war?"

He answered sadly, "Yes, it was."

The boys wanted to know where Daddy had buried Pup but never found out. Try as hard as they could, they never located the burial ground. Boys surely are different from girls. I think if they had known, they would have dug him up just to see if he were still there. I didn't even want to think about such a thing.

Life's experiences helped me to fit together the pieces in the puzzle of life and death. I knew there were many pieces still missing and wondered if I would have to live each one? Or could I just read about it or listen to older, wiser people?

I thought a lot about what people must do to be sure that they would go to heaven. I had heard preachers at church talk about going to hell if we didn't live right. I didn't know where or what that was, except it was a bad word and I thought it must be a very bad place.

When I was younger, a woman at church gave the children an object lesson. She had a piece of thread and asked which of the boys could break the thread. Of course Herbert was the first to raise his hand and broke it easily. Then she put two pieces together and had someone break them. She kept adding one more piece of thread until no

one could break it. She said that was like smoking a cigarette. You could stop after you smoked one, but each time
it became harder and harder to break the habit. I got the
idea that she thought that everyone who smoked cigarettes
would not go to heaven. I didn't think I could agree. Just
maybe she didn't know everything. My Daddy smoked
sometimes and I was certain he was going to heaven.

Later, when I learned the ten commandments, I wondered if anyone who stole things or lied, or all those other
things, would go to heaven. I wanted to be on the safe
side and not do anything to make God unhappy.

In one of my informal talks with God, making sure no
one else heard, I said, "About those vegetables I stole in
the first grade. I'm sorry. You *do* know though, God, I was
just a little girl, so please don't hold it against me." I came
to the conclusion that I wasn't such a bad person, after all.
I didn't smoke cigarettes and I didn't steal like some people
do. I hardly ever lied.

Something happened one day, though, to make me
wonder. It seemed I couldn't keep out of trouble even if I
tried. It was a warm spring day and my friend, Margo, and
I were cutting through an alley on our way home. We saw
a bush full of plump, ripe berries. We were sure that, growing on the alley like that, they must be wild berries. So we
tasted them. They were ripe and truly delicious. We tasted
and tasted again until the bush was empty. How lucky we
were to find such good wild berries before someone else
found them.

Two days later, Margo said that she had overheard her
mother and a friend talking. The friend complained that
she had been saving her blackberries to make jam. When
she went out to pick them, they were all gone. It was a

great mystery. She couldn't understand it. Margo didn't reveal our part in the mystery and neither did I.

This time I hadn't intended taking anything that wasn't mine, so I just explained that to God. I thought they were wild, so it couldn't be counted as stealing. I ignored the little voice that said, *You should at least own up to it and say you are sorry.* That thought was pushed to the back of my mind and I tried to forget all about it.

The next disturbing incident concerned my brother, Herbert. That summer, Herbert and I and our cousin Billy were visiting at Grandma and Grandpa Loring's farm for a few days while Mama and Daddy went to Kansas City. I don't know why they went there.

I had been somewhat worried before this because I knew the boys Herbert went around with used swear words, and I thought Herbert might too. Though I had never heard him say anything worse than *shucks.* Oh yes, there was the time Daddy heard Herbert call someone a fool. Of course, that wasn't swearing, but we weren't allowed to use language like that. Daddy said to him, "Do you know what the Bible says about anyone who calls another a fool?" Herbert didn't know, so Daddy told him it says the person who calls his brother a fool is in danger of hell fire. I guess Daddy didn't want Herbert to get too worried, so he said that God would forgive us for honest mistakes; and as Herbert didn't know it was wrong, He would probably overlook it.

"But," he added, "don't let me hear you use that word again. The next time it wouldn't be an honest mistake." Daddy was just as firm about any of us using slang such as *gosh* and *darn*, or bad grammar such as *ain't.* Our parents didn't want any of us growing up to be vulgar or crude.

Their creed was interesting but not too hard to live with. We were poor but respectable, faded but clean, torn but mended, and we always lived on the right side of the tracks.

The incident I started to tell about was an accident that Herbert had at Grandpa's farm. Herbert and Billy had climbed up into a gnarled, old apple tree. For some reason, Herbert slipped and fell onto a barbed wire fence below. Fortunately, only his leg was cut—but that rather badly. The flesh of the calf, cut to the bone in a three-cornered cut, hung open and blood was all over his leg. Herbert looked down at the cut and said, "Damn." I was as shocked by the word as the cut.

Billy and I helped Herbert get into the house. Grandma said, "My Lord, is he dead?" which is what she always said when anyone got hurt. She saw he wasn't, grabbed a towel and wrapped it around the leg tightly to slow the bleeding. My uncle took Herbert into town to the doctor.

When they came back, Herbert looked rather pale, I thought. Uncle Bob said that was sure some kind of boy. He said, "Doc put in nineteen stitches. Not a thing to kill the pain. And there wasn't a whimper out of Herbie." I was proud of my brother and mighty glad it was him instead of me. I was sure I'd have whimpered or yelled.

Mama and Daddy came back that evening and we told them the whole story and they looked proud too.

What upset me about the whole situation was that Herbert had used that swear word. I wondered if he could ever go to heaven if he talked like that. For several days I thought about it. I didn't see how God could blame him, but still I wondered. I thought maybe I should go see our preacher and ask him. Somehow it didn't occur to me to talk to Mama or Daddy about it. I was afraid of getting

Herbert in trouble. Tattling was definitely out in our code of ethics.

Before I mustered enough courage to go talk with the preacher, something happened which only added to my confusion. Daddy had rented a larger house for us and we were moving. It was only a few blocks away so the move wouldn't change things much. The worst aspect I could think of was that I wouldn't be living across the street from Darryl, but even that wasn't too sad. He had openly declared that Julia Loftus was his girlfriend, so neither Barbara nor I saw much of him. Oh, once in awhile he would come over to our house on Saturday morning and have breakfast with us or get Herbert to go swimming with him in the river. I think, because he was an only child, he liked to be in the noisy atmosphere of our large household.. But he certainly didn't give me any special attention.

Before we moved into the new house, Mama asked that I go over and sweep all the floors and mop the kitchen floor. I didn't do a very good job of mopping, but a fair job of sweeping. Mama and Daddy would be putting down linoleum rugs on most of the floors anyway. I finished my job very quickly and stood by the back door, leaning on the broom.

I considered sweeping the back porch, but thought better of it. *Why waste the time and effort?* I used the extra time to better advantage—day dreaming about the future.

I had already manufactured for myself in my dreams a beautiful home that I would someday have. I knew that when I grew up I would be very rich and have many maids. I was sure there were people in the world who genuinely enjoyed doing housework. They could do mine and enjoy it, and I would do things like helping to care for the sick in hospitals or perhaps teach school. I might spend some of my time cooking, having lots of children and following my husband around the country. He would be frightfully wealthy and travel a lot. He would be very handsome and we would make a delightful couple. But there would always be others to do my housework.

My daydreams were interrupted, as they so often were, by reality. A man was walking up to the back porch. I recognized him immediately. He was our preacher—middle aged, probably as much as thirty years old. He had a friendly smile as he came to the door. "Well now, what are you doing all alone here in this big, empty house?"

I thought I should also be friendly. "Oh, we're moving into this house and I got the job of sweeping the rooms before they bring in the furniture." He walked up and opened the back screen door. As I stepped aside, he came into the room. I wasn't prepared in any way for what happened next. He reached out and put both arms around me.

He said, "You are a very good girl to help your folks like that."

I was uneasy but told myself that some people are friendly in different ways. I was so unwise in the ways of the world that I didn't have sense enough to be afraid. After all, this man was a preacher and weren't preachers supposed to speak for God? I thought, *If there is anyone to be afraid of, it can't be the preacher.*

He gave me a tight squeeze and didn't let go. I was still hanging onto the broom and began to squirm. He said, "You know, you are going to be a very beautiful woman."

Just at that moment, the old truck Daddy had borrowed to move rumbled into the driveway and the preacher dropped his arms and stepped back. He was out the back door before anyone came in the front door. I felt extremely ill at ease.

It wasn't easy for me to talk about awkward situations, so I didn't tell Mama or Daddy. They might think I was making a mountain out of a mole hill, as Daddy used to say; and maybe I was. But I was certain that I had been in the presence of something evil and did not know how to describe it. I was very glad that I had not talked to this preacher about my brother. I knew Mama prayed regularly for each of us children, and I felt assured that she prayed the right prayers and God answered the right answers. That should take care of the growing up and growing better of each of us.

If I learned anything from the whole thing, it was that human beings are not always what they seem. Neither can they always be trusted. After that, I avoided that preacher. I had a girlfriend who went to the Methodist church, and she invited me to visit with her. Mama said I could. Our family didn't belong to the other church, anyway. We were just visiting it.

CHAPTER FIVE

WHERE ARE WE GOING?

The next year, we moved back to Bentley. There were happy times mixed with the hard times. I hung onto every happy moment and wove it into my dreams for tomorrow. My father worked only occasionally—for money, that is. Mostly, he either cleared other people's land to get wood for fuel to keep us warm or was paid in food which kept us from starving.

Many other families with fewer children were even worse off than we. There weren't many regular, steady jobs. Some fathers managed to drown their troubles temporarily in cheap, bootleg whiskey. From listening to Mama and Daddy talk, I discovered why we never had alcohol in our house—aside from the cost of it, of course.

When Daddy was a boy, his father had been an alcoholic who was ordinarily a very kind father. When Grandpa tired of everyday life, he went on a drinking binge and became a different person. I couldn't imagine this of my quiet, plodding grandfather as I saw him at his daily gardening. I wondered when and why he quit drinking. I never really knew him because he seldom spoke.

My father, as a very small boy, was sent to live on a farm with his grandparents. He became homesick and lonely. Because of this, he had decided that he would never drink and spoil someone else's life.

Daddy sometimes told us stories of his childhood, which we called the *olden* days. He learned to work hard on the farm and had no companions his own age. Perhaps that is why he enjoyed all of us so much. He said that in the evenings he sat behind the old woodstove in the kitchen and played the violin. As a boy, he had taught himself to play it. He could play almost any instrument by ear.

And so, on cold winter evenings, Daddy entertained us children by playing the violin. He had never learned the classics, but he played all the old World War I tunes. I remember he played "There's a Long, Long Trail Awindin'," and Mama would say, "Don't play that. It makes me feel sad." He knew a lot of hymns and the faster, square-dance pieces. I don't think he cared so much for the country fiddlin' kind of music, although he played it sometimes at our request. We always asked him for "Turkey in the Straw" and "Bugs in the Buttermilk." Then we would ask for the latest contemporary tunes. If he had heard them, he could play them—at least to our satisfaction. As long as Daddy would play, we would listen. We often spread a blanket on the floor and everyone sat on it with Daddy in a chair. I usually had one of the younger children on my lap. Mama sat in a rocking chair mending, crocheting or just smiling, remembering a time long ago before any of us.

Sometimes Mama would call one of the boys to come shell some popcorn which she would pop as her contribution to the festivity of the evening. At times like that we felt very rich. No one minded that there hadn't been meat on the table for over a week, or that we were using Elks' Lodge bacon grease on our bread instead of butter.

Mama always said we shouldn't complain, but be thankful that we had something. She said the Lord always provides what we need for right now, and the next day is His anyway, so He'll take care of what we need then.

We had an uncle who worked at the Elks' Lodge. He wasn't really an uncle. He was a friend of my daddy's sister. But that is another story. Anyway, this friend, Fred was his name, was in charge of the kitchen at the Elks' and he would save the bacon grease for us rather than throw it out. He also saved some really choice leftover food for us. Once there was a part of a beef roast. Mama made hash for three days out of that. One day "Uncle" Fred asked Daddy to come get some things that had been left over from a big dinner the night before. Daddy came home with two boxes full of leftover fried chicken and potato salad. The week had been a particularly lean one for us and we were all eager to dig into this treat.

But it was not to be. Daddy closed the lids on the boxes and said to Mama, "You know, I've been thinking about this. It may be safe, but it may not be. None of this was in the ice box last night, and that kitchen was hot and steamy. I don't think we will ever be so poor that we need to take chances with the children's health. What do you think?"

71

Mama looked around at all of us. We didn't know as much as Daddy and Mama about poisoned food and she could see we were all visibly disappointed. It must have been hard for her to say, "We aren't going to starve without it."

So Daddy threw it out and some neighborhood dogs had a banquet. I don't think any of them died.

I was more than a little bitter thinking about people who could afford to waste so much and not even notice it. I had heard that only wealthy business men were invited to join the Elks' and that there was a lot of drinking of expensive, bootleg liquor there. I thought it must be as evil a place as Grandma once said the nuns' convent was.

And that was about the time I began to question some of the stories about the convent. A friend, Mary Stater, went there twice a week to work for the sisters. She was one of a family of four girls whose mother had died. Her grandmother took care of them and managed to feed the family by taking in washing and going out to do whatever small jobs she could get working for rich people. The two older girls did housework, also, whenever they could get it. But work was scarce. I considered the Staters truly poor.

I couldn't understand why the nuns had Mary work for them when there were so many of them to do the work. I suppose they pitied this motherless family. Mary asked me to go with her one day after school. She said that she had permission from Sister to bring a friend. I could just watch and wouldn't get paid for it.

I was so curious to see what was behind those foreboding brick walls that I wouldn't have missed the opportunity to visit. Mary took me around the building and in through the back gate. We walked down a garden path.

There were flowers and shrubs everywhere. We walked under a shaded grape arbor. Convenient benches were placed invitingly in the garden. Beside one of these was a niche with a small figure of Mary, the mother of Jesus.

My friend, Mary, said that she had stolen one of these figures and no one knew about it. She thought she might sometime take another one. I told her stealing was a sin. She replied that since she wasn't Catholic and her name was Mary also, she didn't think it mattered.

I followed Mary through a back door of the convent and down some stone steps to a basement room. It was furnished with a few tables and benches. I wondered what they used it for. Mary took a broom from the corner and began sweeping the floor. She said Sister had told her to sweep the floor and dust the furniture in this room today.

Mary worked for awhile and I wandered around looking at the pictures on the wall, some books on a bookshelf and another niche with a figure of Jesus Christ on the cross. I didn't like this because it showed blood dripping from His hands and feet and from the crown of thorns on His head. In our church, we didn't see many pictures of Christ hanging on the cross; just in some of the story books and I always hurried past that page. I decided I liked our pictures better, which showed Him teaching the little children, or the one of the empty tomb and two angels guarding it.

I especially liked one which showed Jesus ascending up to heaven, with all His disciples standing there on that mountain watching him go. I often thought how surprised they must have been. But it gave me a good feeling knowing He went to heaven that way. Sometimes I heard Mama and someone from the church talking about Jesus coming back again that same way. I wasn't sure if I felt good about that or not. I hoped He didn't come until I had a chance to do a lot of the things I still wanted to do. Especially having some of my dreams fulfilled—the ones that had to do with marrying someone very rich and good to me—and having babies of my very own; now I *did* hope I would get to do that.

Eventually, just as Mary was putting the dustcloth and broom away, I looked up to see one of the nuns coming down the inside stairway on the far side of the room. I took a deep breath. I hadn't ever been this close to a nun before. But she had a nice smile. She was carrying a tray with food for us which she set down on the table. She asked Mary to introduce her friend. Mary introduced me to Sister Anne Catherine. I felt rather self-conscious. I never knew what to do with introductions.

She seemed to understand, though, and said, "I'm glad you came today. Now you girls must be hungry. Sister Theresa just finished baking bread and sliced some for you. Sit down here and enjoy it while I go get some money to pay Mary."

There were two tall glasses of cold milk and generous slices of warm bread spread with peanut butter. I was amazed that a nun could bake bread that tasted as good as Mama's. Sister Anne Catherine was soon back with Mary's money, and as she gathered the empty dishes she said, "Come back some time, Bonnie May." We told her goodbye and went out through the garden. It was so peaceful and quiet out there I wished I had time to sit on one of the benches for awhile; but knew I mustn't, for Mama had told me to be home in time for supper.

Mary said she thought the next time she came she would take one of the little statues to add to her collection. I didn't see how she could steal anything from the sisters who had been helping her. I enjoyed my visit and concluded that if that convent was the devil's residence, so were a lot of other places. Maybe the devil didn't actually need a building to live in. Could it be he was everywhere?

Unlikely as it seemed to me then, maybe the devil even showed up sometimes in my own happy home. Could it be the devil that made us children fight or do some of the other wrong things we did? But I didn't like to think about it. So I thought instead of how lucky Mary was to earn fifteen cents.

I thought about the time Mama had given me fifteen cents to go to the store to buy some navy beans. As usual, I was dreaming about other things—mostly about the future—and forgot why I had been sent to the store. I asked for fifteen cents worth of clothespins. When I got home, Mama was unhappy with me and said, "Bonnie May, why don't you keep your mind on what you are doing? Now take these clothespins back and get some beans or we won't have any supper."

I hated to have to do it—admit my mistake, that is— but I knew I must. Unless I could talk Herbert into going for me. He never seemed to be self-conscious about anything. I looked around the yard for him, but he was nowhere to be found, so I started to the store. When I got there, the usual group of old men were sitting around the pot-bellied stove talking, whittling and spitting tobacco juice in a spittoon on the floor. I hurried past them to the counter and plopped down the clothespins with the explanation that Mama wanted beans instead of clothespins.

One of the tobacco-spitters laughed and said, "Yep, reckon yore daddy couldn't feed all them young'ns' clothespins."

And someone else said, "If times get any worse they may have to start eating clothespins." They all laughed.

I turned very red and wished the grocer would hurry. He handed me the package of beans and said, "Thank you, Bonnie May." I hurried out of the store before I realized that I should have been the one to say "Thank you." It seemed to me that everything I did around adults made me look foolish.

But never mind. I seldom worried for long about my embarrassments. There was always something else to think about.

Helping Mama prepare meals was one of the things I truly enjoyed doing even though I despised all other forms of housework. It was a challenge to see what could be done with large quantities of vegetables and not much else. We lived from Grandfather Johnson's garden. My grandmother sent us boxes and bags of tiny, new potatoes, carrots, asparagus, turnips, beets and whatever else was in season.

Grandfather grew the vegetables and had a daily route in town to sell what he grew. Every summer morning, while it was still cool and the vegetables were fresh, he drove the route with his horse and wagon. He sold enough to take care of Grandma and an unmarried aunt who lived with them. When he returned from his route, the leftover vegetables were sent to us.

Of course, in the winter there weren't many fresh vegetables except potatoes and parsnips. Sometimes there would be turnips and beets in the cellar where they had been stored in boxes of dirt. When Daddy had work in the fall, he bought a bushel or two of apples.

The foods we had to buy were flour in 100-pound bags, sugar and milk. Also, oleo margarine—never butter. Only the babies had milk to drink. The rest of us got some in puddings, gravies or creamed vegetables.

Sometimes when a relative had butchered they would give us some of the rendered lard, a hog's head or a sow belly. Mama made head cheese, and that was one of the things I never learned to enjoy. From the sow belly, however, we could have many a well-flavored pot of navy beans. The meat rind was good to chew, but you had to watch for bristly hair that hadn't been scraped off. Usually the little nipples were still there.

I never tired of the navy beans. Mama seasoned them differently from the way some people did. There was the right amount of salt and pepper and a small amount of sugar. I did tire, though, of the many meals of pancakes. When there was nothing else to prepare, Mama could always stir up pancake batter. Even if we had no shortening, she managed. She taught me how to cut a potato in two and rub it on the griddle to keep the pancakes from sticking to the pan. When we had money enough we bought a gallon bucket of syrup. Other times we made our own syrup by scorching some sugar in a pan and then pouring water and more sugar into it and letting it boil until it was thick.

The meal we all loved most, I think, was fried potatoes. If we had bacon grease and potatoes, we would peel and slice potatoes to fill two large iron skillets. I always volunteered to stir the potatoes so that I could prematurely sneak some of the extra crisp slices.

Except for holidays, we seldom had meat, vegetables, potatoes and a dessert all at one meal. The few desserts we had consisted of canned fruit or pudding. Sometimes there was a birthday cake.

During some of our worst times, the nation was also having its worst times. All of us listened on the radio to President Roosevelt's fireside chats. There seemed to be hope when we heard him talk. He promised so many things. And, of course, we gave him full credit when, along with many other needy families, we were issued coupons for food.

Every two weeks Daddy picked up the government food. Our diets became better balanced. There were cans of beef that Mama made gravy from, and we ladled it over either boiled potatoes or homemade bread. We were introduced to grapefruit juice. None of us children had tasted it before and didn't care much for it at first. After a while, it tasted pretty good, and we drank large quantities of it. There was powdered milk which really tasted bad, but was all right for cooking.

The poorer we got, the prouder I got. It was a defense mechanism, but it really didn't help much. When Daddy brought home the food allotments, my pride didn't suffer because no one knew the difference. But there were clothing allotments, and they really made me feel sick. School shoes had always been a problem in our family because there were so many of us. One pair didn't last all year. Many times, Herbert and I folded cardboard to put inside our shoes so rocks wouldn't come through the hole in the bottom. When it rained or snowed, we replaced the cardboard more often.

I never missed school because of not having shoes, but often worried that it might happen. When I told Mama of my worries she repeated her usual answer, "Yes, I know and I am praying about it. But don't borrow tomorrow's troubles. God expects us to consider only the troubles we face right now, today."

So when the government issued coupons for shoes, it was a mixed blessing and curse for me. I hated going to the shoe store with my brothers and sisters and sitting in a row while the clerk fitted each of us. I was sure everyone in town was walking by saying, "Those poor, poor Johnson children. The government has to buy their shoes."

At one time in my early teens, I was visiting Grandma Loring for a weekend. I was the first grandchild and considered myself her favorite, so I spent as much time with her as I could. She always seemed to enjoy talking with me. I liked talking with her except when she wanted to talk about what the Bible said. That sometimes made me uncomfortable because I hadn't made up my mind yet to do everything it said. I wasn't certain that what Grandma and Mama and the people from our church thought it said was really what it meant. I reasoned that so long as I didn't fully understand what the Bible said God wouldn't strike me dead with lightning for not obeying. I had begun to recognize some inconsistencies in the way some other "Christian" people talked and the way they lived. Not Grandma and Mama. I truly respected them.

This particular day, as Grandma and I were talking, Grandma happened to notice my shoes were getting shabby. She said, "Bonnie May, I think it is time for you to have a new pair of shoes."

I answered, "Oh Grandma, I just don't want any more of those poor-people government shoes. I'll stick in some more cardboard."

She laughed a little and said she didn't blame me. She went into the other room and came back with a Sears, Roebuck catalog. She turned to the shoe section and said,

"Now, pick a pair and we'll send for them." That was the most exciting moment of my week. I chose a pair of brown leather oxfords with crepe rubber soles. Crepe rubber soles were a very new thing and not many people had them yet.

Grandma insisted we also order a pair of silk stockings. Some of the girls were just beginning to wear them to school instead of heavy ribbed ones. I expected to wait a couple of years. Mama said sixteen was soon enough for silk stockings. Grandma wanted to order some of the ones that had a fancy design down the back seam. I wasn't so sure but didn't want to hurt her feelings, so I said, "Well, maybe just one pair."

I was proud to wear my new crepe, rubber-soled oxfords. Some of my school friends from the west end of town admired them and I felt momentarily prosperous. I didn't wear the silk stockings for a while because they seemed too different from any I had seen at school. Eventually, I had to wear them when my other stockings were worn out and I didn't get any compliments. One girl did say, "Those are kind of funny looking."

People gave Mama large boxes of old clothing and she did wonderful things with them. She could take a man's old suit apart and make two or three pair of Sunday trousers for the boys. We girls were always well dressed in made-over dresses and coats. The things which had been given to us were usually from more well-to-do families. Many of our friends at school couldn't afford clothing of such expensive material as ours. Mama sometimes used patterned flour sacks to make our summer dresses, the boys' shirts and all of our underwear. Some of the girls, whose fathers had regular jobs, had silk underwear. I never had any and after one incident with my cousin, Barbara Jean, told myself I didn't care.

I was invited to Sunday dinner and to stay overnight with Barbara Jean. I visited the Methodist church with her Sunday morning. The dinner that my aunt prepared was very good. They had roast beef with mashed potatoes and gravy. To me, the real delight was a jello salad. They had a new Frigidaire and could have jello even in hot weather. Most people at least had ice boxes, but we used the cellar to keep food. Not that much needed to be kept for long, the way my brothers ate. We couldn't afford to buy ice most of the time.

After the dishes were done, Barbara Jean and I went into her bedroom to play with her paper dolls. Opening a dresser drawer, she said, "I have something to show you." She took out three new pair of silk underpants—one white pair and two pink pair. I admired them and said she was very lucky to have three new pair at once. She shrugged as she replied, "Oh, Mama always buys several pair at a time. They don't last long, you know." I didn't know. She added rather carelessly, "When these are worn out, you will probably get them. I'll put them in with the old clothes Mama gives to your mama."

I was suddenly so filled with anger that I couldn't think of anything to say. Finally, my pride came to the rescue. I also shrugged as I answered quietly, "Don't bother, Barbara Jean. I don't think I'd want them." I was hoping she would be as insulted as I had been, but she didn't seem to be.

She just scooped up the underwear, stuffed them back in the drawer and said, "Oh, all right, let's go play a game."

It was interesting to me that many of the children from the north end of town showed no signs of poverty. Though the United States Congress had repealed Prohibition, Kansas stayed "dry" and Kansas bootleggers continued to prosper. Their children fared well so far as food and clothing were concerned, but they were never admitted to the social circles of the west-end children. Just as I personally clung to my pride through the hard times of the Great Depression, so the town of Bentley preserved its status symbols. I was on the edge of the upper circle, but seldom included. Neither did I make friends with anyone from the "wrong side of the tracks." There was a rung on the ladder for people like us—the very poor but very proud. We could share that rung only with those who were just like us. I didn't think much about the ones below, but often resented the ones above.

Such was my attitude when our ninth child was born. He was named William Joseph. He was, of course, to be Billy Joe—our sixth boy. I remember thinking, *I wish I could grow up and get away from here.* We didn't need any more mouths to feed government-allotted food. Or any more feet to wear government shoes. What was going to happen to our family? Mama worked so hard. The last time she had any new clothes had been two years ago when the war veterans got a soldier's bonus. Daddy bought Mama a new dress and a new hat.

The bonus was probably the most money our family ever had at one time, but there were so many bills to be paid that it didn't change our lives at all. Mama no longer had a wedding ring. They had to sell it. Daddy had sold his violin. He had a harmonica and a Jew's harp but wasn't often in the mood to perform for us. When he occasionally would pick up the harmonica, the music he played was rather mournful—probably the way he felt at the time.

The only thing we had to remind us of the bonus was Mama's new hat. It was a beautiful yellow straw with a large, floppy brim. Mama looked like an angel when she put on that hat. I think she felt quite elegant then, for she stood a little straighter and smiled a little more when she wore it.

One Sunday afternoon, Daddy said, "All of you get cleaned up. We are going for a drive. We'll take a picnic lunch for supper and then stop by the fairgrounds to see if the circus has started setting up yet." Ringling Brothers, Barnum & Bailey Circus was to be in Bentley the next week.

It didn't take us long to get ready. I got ready in a hurry so that I could help with the younger ones, and in no time at all we had squeezed into our old touring car. We older ones got in the back seat first, and the younger ones sat on our laps. It was all quite orderly because each of us knew where we were assigned to sit. Riding in layers like that didn't bother any of us. We all managed to see out the windows.

Mama had put on her new dress and her new yellow hat. Daddy teased her, "You'd better hang onto that hat." She said, "Don't worry, I will." So for most of our drive Mama was holding onto her hat. Our old car didn't go very fast, but the wind blew hard without any help from us. Kansas winds blow hot or cold most of the time. Daddy drove up some country roads we hadn't seen before and some we had. Twice we passed farms of people we knew and waved gaily to them. Once, Daddy pointed to our right to the Republican River. The winter snows and heavy spring rains had swollen the river to twice its natural size.

Just then, Jimmy Lee took a large, fuzzy caterpillar out of his pocket and dropped it on Dora Lynne. Her shriek caused Mama to let go of her hat and look around. The hat blew off and sailed gracefully through the air, gliding down onto the water in the center of the rushing river. Daddy stopped the car. We all got out and stood, watching sadly as our symbol of prosperity became smaller and smaller and finally disappeared in the distance.

"Where will it go?" Edna June wondered.

"Probably to the next town and on through so fast we'd never catch it," Daddy said. As he herded all of us back into the car, I looked at Mama. She swallowed really hard and said, "Oh well, who needs a hat anyway?" We were quiet the rest of the afternoon. Dora Lynne forgot to tell on Jimmy Lee.

After Billy Joe was born, Mama was sick for what seemed a long time. I came home from school at noon each day and prepared the noon meals for the children, checked on Mama and the baby, and stacked the dishes in the dishpan. After school, I hurried home to wash the dishes, wash some diapers—or as we called them, *diddies*—and get supper ready for the family.

Dora Lynne and Edna June helped with the baby. They soon learned how to change diddies and to fix his bottles. I bossed my brothers around unmercifully. I insisted that they help with the housework. When they didn't do what I told them to do, I either grabbed them by the back of the neck and pinched hard until they did or I told Daddy on them. I think they despised me. I probably despised my lot in life at the moment. I didn't boss Herbert because I couldn't. He managed to be elsewhere after school most of the time.

On Saturdays I baked bread for the family. For me this was no chore because I truly enjoyed doing it. By afternoon, I usually had time to get away by myself with a book or to think about life. There was a large, old tree in our backyard and I often climbed up there to hide out in the leafy branches where no one could see me. One day on one of the high limbs, I discovered a robin's nest with three little blue eggs.

Each day after school, I climbed up to check on that would-be family. When the eggs were finally hatched I shared some of the excitement with that mother robin. In a few days, she left the nest frequently to find food for her babies. One day when I climbed up to look, all of the tiny birds were gone. I couldn't understand it. They weren't old enough yet to fly.

I looked down and just below me curled up in the crotch of the tree was a huge bull snake. I screamed and made a flying leap from the branch where I sat. It was a miracle I didn't break an arm or leg. I saw Herbert coming around the corner of the house and yelled for him to come kill the snake. He said, "Bonnie May, you know a bull snake won't hurt you."

"Well, this one just ate three baby robins, and he was looking at me with his beady eyes. He about scared me to death." I ran into the house and left Herbert to decide whether to kill the snake or carry him off somewhere. I don't know what he did, but I never climbed my favorite tree again. In fact, it was no longer my favorite tree.

I don't think Mama had a fear of snakes, but Grandma Loring was as fearful of them as I. A few years before on the farm, she had been sitting outside in the sun churning butter. She had a tall crockery churn with a wooden plunger. She would sit on the chair and move the plunger up and down until the cream in the churn turned to butter.

On this particular day, she was singing in time with the splashing of the cream and enjoying the sun on her back. My uncle had a little rat-terrier dog named Joe who liked to sleep at Grandma's feet whenever she sat down anywhere. So, when she thought she felt Joe at her feet, she didn't even look down. Soon, something didn't seem right and she looked down to see a bull snake curling around her ankles. Her scream that followed was heard distinctly by Granddad as he worked in an adjoining field. He left his horses, ran to the fence and jumped superhumanly over a six-foot gate. Within a minute or so he was in the yard.

Grandma had disentangled herself and was inside the house with the screen door hooked. The snake was slithering away from all the hubbub. Grandma was still so shaken she insisted that Granddad go after the snake and kill it. Mostly, farmers didn't kill bull snakes unless their wives insisted because this species is useful for killing rats and mice and other small animals that can harm the crops.

Gradually, Mama began to feel better and took over the household chores. My conscience didn't bother me when I disappeared for half a day at a time with a book. This was my escape from the unsettled world, our unsettled family and my unsettled soul. With a book I was someone else, somewhere else. That's what I thought I wanted.

Chapter Six

The In-between

I couldn't know it, but for the most part, my inner con-
flicts were ordinary growing pains. One day I planned for
a beautiful, problem-free future and the next, I longed to
keep everything just as it was.

I was ashamed of my parents for being so poor. And then
ashamed of myself for blaming my parents. For the present,
I felt I couldn't do anything right; but for the future, I knew
there was nothing I couldn't do or be if I set my mind to it.
Teachers told us this repeatedly, and I believed them.

I was too old to cry about our troubles, but too young to
laugh at them. I was like a trapped bird who wanted to fly.
There was a restless flopping of wings without getting anywhere. Inside me were fears and guilts and panics and worries. On the outside, I smiled and laughed too loudly, talked

too much and tried to cover up everything that was boiling inside.

It was my first year at junior high school. Junior high and high school were combined in one building. I had become a very small duck in a seemingly large puddle. Sometimes I enjoyed the anonymity because I was so awkward and didn't want to be noticed. Other times, I longed to be a very important someone. I felt I was in a maze with no way out.

Before long, I discovered that the entire seventh grade was made up of boys and girls more or less like me. Each was somewhat uncertain of his worth and place in life. Such identification with one another made it easy to stand around for many hours after school and brag about accomplishments, tell dirty stories and use coarse language. This didn't really prove anything except that we were willfully and independently doing something our folks would not approve of. The education I received outside the classroom was new and strange. I don't know how my parents had managed it, but my life had been so sheltered that much of the language I heard was completely foreign to me.

At home, I did as little work as possible and, pretending to spend hours reading or studying, dreamed large dreams. Romance was threaded in and out of my dreams. Not with the squeaky-voiced, pimply-faced school boys, but always with a shadowy, strong someone who was just waiting for me to come along.

He would sweep me off my feet, we'd marry and I would never wear another pair of government shoes, nor eat from another tin of government beef. We would have five healthy, beautiful, well-dressed children who would take piano and ballet lessons. If he came along soon enough, I might not even finish high school. But that part of the dream was fuzzy and faded almost as soon as it appeared. It didn't fit with one goal which seemed very, very important. The goal of finishing high school.

Mama had said she wanted every one of her children to get a high-school diploma. When she said it, you thought there was something magic and mystical about it. You became determined not to disappoint her.

Neither Daddy nor Mama had gone to high school. Mama had only completed the sixth grade and Daddy the eighth grade. Both, however, had read and studied extensively on their own. It would have been difficult for an outsider to guess they weren't college graduates. When Daddy was working on a project he didn't understand, such as refinishing an old violin, he went to the library and checked out every book he could on the subject. Both Mama and Daddy instilled in us an interest in poetry, literature and science which motivated us to want to know more.

I had many fears—some undefined, some quite definite. I worried about not having food, clothing or school books. I worried about losing my parents. I had heard of orphans and wondered what we would do if anything happened to Mama and Daddy.

That winter Daddy did become quite ill. He was weak and unable to work much. He began to spit up blood. Mama, who didn't cry often in front of us, cried. She was certain he had T.B. If a doctor said you had tuberculosis, that was the same as signing your death warrant.

We had known an elderly man who made furniture from willow branches he cut along the river. He soaked the supple boughs in water and bent them to the desired shapes. He then painted the pieces of furniture black and trimmed them with gold. My brother, Herbert, and I had been fascinated when he allowed us to watch the painting process. We wanted to try putting on the gold decoration, but he said gold paint was very expensive and also quite dangerous if you breathed too near it.

We missed seeing the old man for a few days and then noticed that some unfamiliar people came into his house and carried out all the furniture he had been working on. When we asked Mama what was happening, she told us that the old man had died of T. B.

A year or so after that, another neighbor, a lady down the street who lived with her daughter, was said to have tuberculosis. Every evening she went for a walk around the block. Mama said the exercise was good for her. She died anyway.

Herbert and I thought T.B. must be about the worst disease there was—except, of course, polio, but that was only a child's disease…wasn't it?

When it was suspected Daddy might have tuberculosis, all of us became very solemn. Herbert and I gravely considered the possibilities of life without a father. The doctor gave Daddy some tests and we waited a very long time for the results. It was not tuberculosis. We never knew what it was, but after he found he didn't have the dreaded disease, Daddy began to get better.

I quit worrying about the family and resumed my daydreams about the future. I checked out library books which had romantic titles. Mysteries no longer interested me. I loved sad or romantic poetry. I even borrowed a few *True Confession* magazines from a friend. Mama didn't read them and I didn't risk asking her if I could read them. I soon tired of those, also. I couldn't identify with the plots.

The happiest and most exciting times were centered around school. I joined the Girls' Athletic Association at school and took part in after-school athletics. In gym, I learned to play basketball. Being tall for my age, I became one of the star players. It helped to be somebody. Our team was asked to play an exhibition game in the gym one evening and my spirits were higher than they had been for a long time. When we practiced they let us play in our socks, but for the game we must wear gym shoes. I didn't own any.

I decided to swallow my pride and borrow a pair of shoes from Barbara Jean. The pair she loaned me were a bit too large for her and a bit too small for me. It was humiliating to have to ask her, but the fame balanced the shame, and I told myself it was worth it this time.

I couldn't attend the football games because we seldom had the price of admission. But the highlight of the week was Thursday evening when the entire school turned out for a pep rally. The seventh graders were there in one large gang. We practiced all the yells, followed the band down the middle of Main Street and ended up at the town theater. There was always the idea that we would crash the theater and see a free movie. It never quite worked out that way. Each time, the manager came out and explained why we couldn't come in free, and we would break up and go home mumbling, "Wait till next week."

There had been a series of dust storms which left our houses and school classrooms covered in a thin layer of dust. One Friday morning, about ten o'clock, our teacher got up from his desk and turned on the classroom lights. We looked out the window and saw that the dust was blowing so thickly that it was dark as dusk.

As the morning wore on, it continued to get darker. At 11:30, the principal called a special assembly and we all filed into the auditorium. He announced that no one was to start for home for their noon meal. He said if anyone wished to do so they could borrow money from the school for lunch and pay it back next week. Most of the students were quite happy with the decision. There was a circus atmosphere everywhere.

In our cooking class that morning, we had made date muffins and some of us girls were saving several of them to take home with us. We decided to eat those and forget the school lunch. I knew I couldn't pay back the money anyway, so I was relieved that everything worked out so neatly. We enjoyed the whole day. We didn't know, of course, that what we considered an adventure was a tragedy to many farmers.

The wind died down in time for us to go home from school, but there was still a dust cloud overhead which obscured the sun and caused the world to look unreal. The dust had drifted and piled like snow. Later that evening, Daddy told Mama that it had to be Oklahoma dust because it was so red. He said, "They must not have any topsoil left. We have it all."

There was much talk about the explosion of the hydrogen gas balloon called the *Hindenberg*. Thirty-six people were killed. When I heard that I recalled seeing the stuntman parachute to his death, and I remembered how sad I had been when Tommy Bob had died. Death and foreboding occupied my thoughts. I went to church and sat through long, boring sermons which added to my unrest. I tuned out the sermon and, while there, thought about anything else I could.

At intervals, I heard the preacher say, "But I must hasten on." He never did—hasten, that is. His sermons lasted for an hour and a half, and I didn't think anything he said applied to me. Sometimes, though, I listened more carefully when he said, "You are either going to heaven or hell." *That must apply to everyone.* I wasn't too sure I was good enough for heaven. I believed in hell and knew I didn't want to go there. *Try not to think about it.*

One night I lay in bed, not able to go to sleep for fear I might die and go to hell. Everyone else in the family was sound asleep. Dora Lynne, who didn't worry much about anything, was occupying two-thirds of our bed with her feet planted firmly in the middle of my back. She had no trouble sleeping. Finally, I slipped out of bed and went out into the hall and into my parents' bedroom. Mama always heard every sound we children made and so I didn't have to wake her. She whispered, "What's the matter, honey?"

"Will you pray with me?" She was out of bed and we both padded barefoot into the front room and knelt down in our flannel nightgowns before the sofa.

"What do you want to pray about?"

"I don't know." It was hard to communicate such personal thoughts. My fears suddenly seemed very silly and I waited while Mama prayed that the Lord would help me sleep comfortably and give me peace of mind. Then we got up, she gave me a little hug and I went back to bed. I was soon sound asleep. Nothing had changed, but I assumed that since Mama had such a direct line to heaven, I needn't worry anymore.

I didn't think much more about hell but became troubled about other things. One of those was the disillusionment I was experiencing with my favorite grandmother. I saw a side of Grandma Loring, the model Christian, which was perplexing. I had, for several years, shelved the things she had said about the Catholics. Now it came up again.

Uncle Bob had a girlfriend who was Catholic. To hear Grandma carry on, nothing worse could have happened to

Uncle Bob. We had a family picnic at Grandma's the following Friday which was a holiday and there were loads of fried chicken. The girl, whose name was Delia, didn't eat any of the fried chicken because it was Friday; and Grandma later told Mama that was worse than being a heathen. I don't know if she meant not eating her chicken or being a Catholic. I rather liked Delia because she laughed a lot and had fun with all of us, except Grandma. I think she was a little afraid of her.

While I was mulling over whether it was fair to feel unfriendly toward Delia, another new and startling prejudice surfaced. In our small town there was one black family. They were very respectable people who also lived on the east side of town. They had a girl in the grade ahead of me. She and I walked home from school together many days. Her name was Vivian, and I thought she was the prettiest girl I knew.

Vivian had a smooth, light-chocolate complexion and sparkly eyes. But the reason I thought she was so pretty was her dimples. I had, all my life, admired and longed for dimples in my cheeks. Sometimes I would stand before the mirror and push the eraser end of a pencil in my cheek to see if I could create those cute indentations. Of course, the dimples weren't lasting, but they did last long enough for me to see that I would be strikingly beautiful if I had dimples. All Vivian had to do was laugh or smile a little, or just talk and her dimples darted in and out. She was so lucky.

One day, Grandma was visiting at our house and saw us walking home together. As I came in the front door, I heard Grandma say, "Mary, do you let Bonnie May walk home with that nigger girl?" I was shocked by Grandma's remark. Surprisingly enough, Mama and Grandma didn't agree on everything.

Mama said, calmly but firmly, "Vivian is a very nice girl and I would rather Bonnie May walked with her than some."

The real problem was with me. I loved my grandma very much. She was everything a Christian lady should be, I thought, in most every way. But how could she make such a difference in people? I didn't think that God's love was so conditional; and He surely didn't want ours to be, either. I felt very sad when I contemplated the effects that prejudice could have on even good people. I concluded there was much I didn't know. I just didn't like not liking something about my grandma.

It wasn't long until Uncle Bob quit going with Delia. I believe she decided she didn't want to marry a non-Catholic, so there wasn't much point in going with him any longer. Before Grandma had time to say, "Thank you, Lord, for answering my prayers," Uncle Bob met and married another Catholic girl named Mary Alice. They hadn't consulted Grandma and so she didn't have time to pray them out of it.

Granddad Loring got sick and was in bed for many days, and Grandma had all she could do to take care of him. My mother and her two sisters went in to help whenever they could, but it was Mary Alice who did the most. She took in meals, did the washing and ironing, and helped Grandma in many ways. Granddad continued to get worse and we children knew from the conversations we overheard that he was going to die. Mama was at their house one whole day when she came home and told us that Granddad had gone to be with the Lord in heaven. She seemed strangely calm and peaceful, not really unhappy. Oh, there was a sadness there but a very peaceful acceptance.

Mama said that Granddad was ready to die. He had been lying quietly in bed, sometimes moaning because he was in such pain. Suddenly, obviously excited, he sat up in bed. He was saying, "Glory, glory, glory. It is all so glorious here."

They knew he was seeing something none of them could see. When he lay back down he had a peaceful expression on his face. He seemed to go to sleep. The pain was gone. All the lines on his face made by the pain were gone. Mama said she could only feel glad for him. Of course, we would all miss him—Mama, perhaps, most of all.

Herbert and I had spent much time visiting this set of grandparents and we knew nothing would ever be the same. I was glad I hadn't been there when illness made my grandfather so weak. I remembered him as very strong.

Granddad Loring had been a large man, six feet or more, and always seemed to have more strength than he needed for anything. I remembered one surprising incident which had startled him as much as it did Herbert and me. He had milked the cows and left the buckets of milk sitting beside the barn while he went across the barnyard to get something. He looked back and saw one of the farm tomcats approaching the milk buckets. He yelled "Scat," but the cat didn't scat. He reached down and picked up a corncob from the pile beside him. He threw it, intending I'm sure to frighten the cat into running away. His aim was too perfect. The cob hit the cat squarely in the middle of the forehead and that cat dropped dead in his tracks. I mean literally dead.

We children couldn't believe it and Granddad couldn't either. He sort of stammered, "Well, I didn't intend to kill it." We knew he didn't and, much as we hated to see an animal die, we couldn't blame our grandfather. Another time, he picked up a rattlesnake by its tail and swung it hard and fast against a building, crushing its head.

Granddad had always been a hard-working man. Most of his life he was a farmer. When they moved to town, he became a plumber. I had only seen him a few times in a Sunday suit. Almost always he wore bib overalls and heavy work shoes. His hands were rough and callused, with the third finger on one hand missing. Mama said he had lost that finger in an accident with a saw while helping someone cut wood planks.

Though big, strong and seemingly coarse, he was also gentle and kind. He loved children and could not understand anyone mistreating a child. When the little Lindbergh boy was kidnapped, Granddad was as angry as I had ever seen him. He said, "They should take all those people and string them up by their thumbs." I had never heard of that particular form of punishment but considered it an interesting possibility. Someone said something about the punishment fitting the crime.

Mama told us that, at the last, when someone had to be with Granddad all the time, Mary Alice had been there as much as any of the daughters. Grandma may never have felt any more kindly toward the Catholics, but she definitely learned to love one of them in spite of herself.

That spring and summer while I was still in the gap between wanting to play house with dolls but looking forward to my own real children and home, I rode the roller coaster of early teen emotions. Adolescence was not my friend. Valentines were too juvenile, Maybaskets still fun.

Because I helped the younger children with the cutting, pasting and filling with flowers and goodies, I was young and happy when we made Maybaskets. I helped them gather lilacs to put in each one. We went on a violet-hunting excursion. There were a few shady, damp spots under the railroad bridge and behind a shed where we could count on finding the dainty, purple flowers. The violets were so beautiful. The fragrance of the lilacs couldn't be matched. I loved to bury my face in an armload of the sweet-smelling blossoms.

We had a park with a band shell and Maypole. Some of the boys and girls from school had been selected to dance around the Maypole, weaving in and out with the pastel streamers. If done properly, this would result in a beautifully wrapped pole. Someone always made a mistake, but it was fun for everyone. All the townspeople turned out to watch.

This was also the first evening of the weekly band concerts in the park. The concerts continued all summer. It hardly ever rained in the summer. Everyone came to hear the music or just visit with friends. They sat on benches or brought blankets and sat on the grass. There was no age gap; tiny babies up to great grandparents attended.

All of us children walked home from school through the park because it was "as the crow flies," but also because there was usually something to do there—swings and slippery slides or just a casual stroll with friends.

Jimmy Lee went through the park for another reason. Some of the men working on the W.P.A. were always there, leaning on their shovels and looking for any kind of diversion. Jimmy Lee provided it. He soon discovered that if he did acrobatic tricks, mostly standing on his head, the men would give him pennies. Each day he was a few cents richer. The men encouraged him to try handsprings, cartwheels and various other maneuvers like walking on his hands. Jimmy Lee became affluent, but not frugal. He spent the pennies on candy as soon as he could get to the store. I don't think Mama even knew about his endeavors.

The summer was carefree. There were no emotional crises. I slipped back into childhood again as I organized and played games with my brothers and sisters. As usually happens with large families, we attracted many other children, cousins, neighbors and friends. Everyone could count on an exciting time at the Johnsons. The other parents didn't mind because they knew our parents were good people. My parents didn't mind because a large family requires very little supervision. Each child learns very early to be responsible for someone younger.

We all knew the principles by which Mama and Daddy lived and the boundaries we must respect. Discipline inevitably followed a deliberate stepping outside these boundaries. We weren't allowed to lie, steal, swear or *sass* our elders. We had to be around the table at mealtime, hands washed and hair combed.

No matter how little we had to eat, there was always an extra child or two there. There were long benches on either side of the table so more bodies could be squeezed together. The girls were always expected to clear the table and wash the dishes. In the summer that is about all that Mama required of us, except for caring for one another.

There was plenty of time for play. I loved to organize the games and no one seemed to mind, or didn't bother to cross me by saying so. Hide-and-seek was a favorite of everyone. I didn't like being "It"; and since I had appointed myself the official organizer, usually managed to avoid that position.

One hot summer afternoon when Barbara Jean and her little sister, Geneva, came to play, we began a game of Hide-and-seek. Geneva, being the youngest and slowest to say "Not it," was standing facing a tree with her eyes covered and concentrating on her counting. As she could not count past twenty, we scrambled to our hiding places.

She yelled, "Ready or not..."

And six people answered, "Not ready," so she had to begin again.

When Geneva came looking for us she found Dora Lynne and Edna June first. They had hidden together in the tool shed and couldn't resist giggling when she came near. They then helped her look for the others. Herbert and Barbara Jean sneaked in, tapped the tree and yelled, "In free." When they joined the search, the others were soon found. All except me.

I would do anything to prove my superiority. So I hid in the most unlikely place of all: the two-holer outhouse at the back of our lot. I knew they would find me if I just stood inside the door, so I climbed up inside the peaked roof and sat on the rafters, holding my nose. Eva looked in once but didn't look up.

I heard everyone standing in the yard discussing what could have happened to me. Geneva said, "I looked everywhere, even in the toilet."

Barbara Jean asked, "Did you really look in there?"

Geneva replied, "Yes, and I looked down the hole—ugh! No, I looked down both holes and she wasn't there." By this time I was laughing uncontrollably and since I had proved my point, scrambled down and out into the fresh air. No one was especially glad to see me. They just wanted to get on with the game.

We went into the front yard to start another game and saw the ice man coming down the street. We sat down to map our strategy. If we followed him long enough he would cut a large chunk of ice into smaller pieces for his customers. Some small chunks would fall off; those he gave to the children. We knew we shouldn't overwhelm him with so many of us at once or he might not give anyone a piece.

We divided our numbers. We left Barbara Jean with the first group, which was mostly made up of the younger ones. She wasn't allowed to leave Geneva and so that was all right. Several of us would run over to Seventh Street and start following him at the corner of Seventh and Madison. The rest would go to Tenth and Madison and follow him until all of us got ice. Herbert was in charge of this group. He told me he hoped my group was successful before we got to Tenth Street. I assured him we would do our part.

We set our plan in motion and eventually everyone was back sitting under the elm tree in the front yard sucking on a piece of ice. Eddie David dropped his, and it was so small it melted in the dust immediately. I let him have a few licks of mine to keep him quiet. He was a good-natured, little blue-eyed blond. I adored him and he reciprocated by following me everywhere.

There was a one-car train which ran daily between Bentley and Jamesville twenty miles away. Everyone called it the *Doodlebug*. It had a shrill whistle which we could hear as it approached Bentley. Eddie David listened each day for that whistle and one day he lisped, "Thereth the Doo-o-odle bug." I teased him after that by calling him Doodle Bug. He would always say, "No, I'm not. I'm Edward David Johnthon." I thought his lisp was so cute.

The ice interlude was refreshing. We had no ice box because we could seldom afford to buy ice. On the few occasions when Daddy bought a fifty-pound chunk at the city ice house, he would wrap it in newspaper and old rags and put it in the cellar to keep it from melting so fast. When any of the children saw Daddy coming home with ice, they got excited because that meant something fun was going to happen—like homemade ice cream or ice cold lemonade for a picnic.

The week before, Edna June had been the only one to see Daddy come in with ice. Later, she was standing in the back yard with Dora Lynne. She dangled her secret. "You can't guess what I know."

Dora Lynne asked, "What?"

Edna June, who had been twirling a rope and trying to learn how to lasso, looked down to see that Dora Lynne was unsuspectingly standing in the loop. Edna June, with one end of the rope in her hand, answered, "I know how to play a new game."

Dora Lynne was curious. "All right, Edna June, stop acting silly. What's the name of your new game?"

"The game is called The Ice Is in the Cellar," and without warning, Edna June yanked on the end of the rope, tightening the loop around Dora Lynne's ankles and flipped her to the ground. She ran around the house before Dora Lynne could untangle her feet. She was convulsed with laughter, but knew she had better get out of range.

The whole episode ended in a chase around the house, a bit of pounding and Mama pulling them apart with a warning to quit fighting or they'd both get a spanking.

Now, as we sat discussing what to play next, Edna June with a sparkle in her brown eyes and a shake of her red curls, suggested "Let's play The Ice Is in the Cellar."

Dora Lynne lunged toward her and the fight would have started all over again, but Allan Dale—ever the peacemaker—intervened with, "Naw, let's play Statue."

There was instant agreement and we spent the next half hour engrossed in this game. Herbert and I both liked to be "It" in this game. Actually, it took two people anyway. The two would privately decide together what they wanted their statue to resemble. Then one would swing the child with one hand. Each child must stay in the exact position he fell when the statue maker let go of his hand. The other "It" person would decide which of the children most nearly resembled his statue. The winner got to be "It."

We had played until most everyone had been "It" when our aunt came for Barbara Jean and Geneva. They didn't want to go home, but Aunt Corrie said they must. We asked them to come back next week and we would play Statue some more. I told Barbara Jean not to forget to bring her stamp collection. I was starting a butterfly collection and we could work on them together.

We all waved goodbye and then Mama called us inside to get ready for supper. We were having a special treat that evening because Aunt Corrie had brought a burnt-sugar cake. We really liked that cake. I think it had lots of real butter in it.

I was glad the cake wasn't angel food. During the Depression, eggs were so cheap that everyone made angel food cake. For some reason, I had never liked angel food cake or pumpkin pie. Most of the family thought that quite strange. I knew I would never like either, even if eggs got as expensive as fifty cents a dozen. Of course, they would never cost that much.

During supper, Mama and Daddy were talking about school starting and Daddy said, "Well, I made enough helping Mr. Ames painting his house to buy the boys' overalls and the children's school books. But, after we pay the bills, there will just be enough left to get some flour, sugar, lard and oleo."

Mama nodded, "Yes, I know. There won't be anything left for school shoes."

CHAPTER SEVEN

LEAVE US ALONE

Change is always uncomfortable. Suffering the discomforts of a changing world, constantly changing home and a physically changing me, I didn't recognize the important stabilities. My parents' values hadn't varied. Their love for each other and for all of us was as earnest as ever. "The church's one foundation," as my grandmother often sang, was still Jesus Christ our Lord. I was concerned only with my peer group and myself. There I saw considerable change and instability.

I admired poised persons and, thus, longed for sophistication. Reading was ever a great escape. I devoured poetry and discreetly tried composing some of my own, which I hid from everyone who might read it. While some of the girls and boys in the eighth grade turned to coarse and crude language, I poured over the dictionary to learn new words. I practiced saying each word until I was certain the pronunciation was perfect. If we hadn't been so poor, I think I would have become a sophisticated snob.

Mama was a childish word, and so I began saying *Mother* instead. She didn't seem to mind. Herbert, at the same time, had changed to calling our mother *Mom*. Sometimes we called our father *Dad*, but most of the time, for me at least, *Daddy* seemed quite appropriate—possibly because I knew that by putting an arm around his neck and saying plaintively, "Daddy," any request would be granted. Mother saw through my tactics and it was a bit more difficult to get what I wanted from her at times. She gave permission when she felt she should but other times was absolutely immovable.

The physical changes in my body made me tired and self-conscious. I was too tall and too thin and not filled out enough in the right places. I wasn't motivated to study and C-average grades reflected my attitude. The fact that Barbara Jean was getting As and Bs and was learning to play the piano didn't help. Some people had all the luck and that was all right. I would just ignore her. It was easier not to like her than to compete with her.

One day in study hall when I was supposed to be doing my math assignment for the next day, I sat idly jotting down ideas for a play. I belonged to a girls' club which aimed at teaching us the social graces. I looked forward to the weekly, after-school meetings. We were given instructions on proper table settings, names of French foods, skin care and how to have shiny hair. Even what to do if you were presented to the queen of a foreign country.

Our sponsor, the English teacher, Miss Myers, had announced that we would be having an afternoon tea for our mothers in a month and we would discuss what entertainment to have. I thought putting on a play would be fun but didn't know where to look for one; so as the ideas came, I found myself writing a play. I didn't know at the time what *plagiarism* meant, but may have committed it because the play was full of funny stories that I had heard or read— nice clean ones, suitable for mothers and daughters, of course.

When I had finished the play, I took it to Miss Myers. She liked it and, at the next meeting, suggested that we use it and that I direct it. That was fine with me because, while I could talk with the others at our practice sessions, I knew I could never appear before the mothers. I just couldn't cope with stage fright.

The practices were stimulating. I wasn't sure what a director should do, but I helped prepare and set up the props and listen as each person said her memorized lines. The play was called *The Little Red Schoolhouse* and was supposedly a typical day in a country school—complete with water bucket, dipper, individual slates and whatever else we were able to collect.

We were coached also on the social amenities of a formal tea. Hostesses were chosen to pour the tea from borrowed silver pots and to ask, "Lemon?" or, "One lump of sugar or two?" On the day of the tea, the table looked quite elegant with a white cloth, flowers in the center and trays of tiny homemade cookies. Some of us had practiced holding a tea cup with the little finger extended in a crook. Someone said that was how high society drank their tea. These practices were accompanied by much giggling, which we solemnly promised not to do at the tea. We all dressed in our Sunday best dresses.

The mothers began to arrive and they, too, had dressed especially nice for the occasion. Everyone wore a hat and gloves, even my mother. I didn't know she owned white gloves. She must have kept them in her cedar chest where she had some of her own special treasures. I noted that, except for looking a little more tired perhaps, she was as stylish as anyone there.

After the tea and cookies were finished, everyone sat down for the entertainment. There was a piano solo, a song by six of the girls, and then Miss Myers stood up and announced that there would be a play.

She had insisted that I sit beside her until the announcement was made, and I felt extremely embarrassed. She told the mothers that one of the girls had not only written the play but had directed it. She introduced me and I had to stand up while the mothers clapped. I could feel the red creeping up my neck and wished I were anywhere but there. I tried to smile and was glad I didn't have to say anything. While Miss Myers gave the names of the cast, I slipped out to go into the adjoining room to make sure that everyone was ready.

The performance was perfect except that a bucket of water was spilled on the hardwood floor, and it wasn't going to make the janitor very happy. Everyone laughed at the jokes. At the end, Miss Myers had all the cast stand and everyone clapped.

I looked around to see where my mother was standing. As I started toward her, Miss Myers came up with one of the mothers. A west-ender, as we called the people who lived in the "right" part of town. Miss Myers said the play had gone well and then introduced me to the mother, who put out her hand to shake hands. I was startled at the gesture. She was saying something about enjoying the performance. I just looked down at my shoes, certain that whatever I said would be the wrong thing. The woman's daughter came and pulled her mother over to see someone else.

Miss Myers' reprimand was deserved, but hurt nonetheless. She said, "Bonnie May, Mrs. Townsend told you how much she enjoyed the play and you didn't acknowledge it."

I mumbled, "Sorry," and walked over to my mother to tell her that I would be staying for a half hour more to help clear up things.

For a week I writhed inside at how dumb I had acted when given some recognition for my efforts in producing the play. Recognition was what I thought I wanted, but when I got it I didn't know what to do with it. I wanted to crawl in a hole. I wondered if I would ever be a poised person. Maybe I would die young and it would never matter. People would have to say, "She was such a beautiful girl. Wonder why she had to die so young?" Or something to that effect.

The next Sunday at church, we had a visiting preacher who thundered and pounded the pulpit. He convinced me that dying was not what I wanted either—at least not a martyr's death. He told of a man who had been buried alive up to his neck. The man was commanded to deny his faith, but would not. With each opportunity to deny and each avowal that he wouldn't, another shovelful of dirt was dropped in the hole around him. Finally, he had only one more opportunity and still did not deny his faith.

I pictured myself being covered with dirt and gasping for air and choking to death as the last shovel of dirt was dropped around my face. I told myself, *No, thank you. I don't want to die and if that is what it means to be a Christian, I don't want that either. Someone else will have to do it.*

After that, I avoided church whenever I could. Of course it wasn't always possible to get out of going, but when I went I found it was easy to tune out the sermon and think about other things—school and friends my own age. Sometimes I could get by with going to Sunday school and not staying for church. The teacher, however, was boring and unreal.

Sister Evans—we called our members *brother* and *sister*—always wore a long, black dress. She wore high-top button shoes which had been out of style for many years. We thought since hers were in such good condition she must have saved the same pair for Sundays for the past fifty years; and, of course, she would have an old-fashioned button hook at home to button the shoes. She wore an out-of-date hat over her gray hair, which was twisted into a tight bun in the back. Perched on her nose was a pair of wire-rimmed glasses. She considered many things a sin and I think style was one of them.

Some of the other "sins" she taught us about were: movies, short hair, short skirts, lipstick, nail polish, dancing, smoking and drinking. Sister Evans was married to a man named Will who was a retired preacher. He did almost everything his wife told him to do. They never had any children. I always supposed it was because they were married rather late in life until I overheard my aunt and mother talking one time. They said that Will and Jessamine had gone together for five years when Jessamine's mother became ill. The mother, on her deathbed, told them they could marry but exacted a promise that they would never have children.

Fortunately, our mother didn't take Sister Evans and her list of *don'ts* too seriously, and neither did we. Mother always stressed the positive side of faith. Thus, we were able to avoid an open rebellion against God Himself.

One of our preachers had three daughters and two sons whom Sister Evans took it upon herself to help "nurture in the Lord." She discovered that one of the older girls had attended a school dance and she went at once to have a talk with the preacher's wife.

One of the girls told me afterwards that her mother listened quietly and then looked Sister Evans right in the eye and said, "Now I want you to understand something: My husband and I have been given these children and the responsibility to bring them up as God directs us. If I ever hear that you have mentioned dancing or anything else of that nature to one of my girls, you will have to answer to me. Is that clear?" Needless to say, Sister Evans was taken aback. I suspect this might not have been the first time she had interfered, but she had great respect for the preacher and his wife and so far as I know left their children strictly alone after that.

My second year in junior high I was able to attend the football games because I had a small job. Mother had heard about an elderly blind lady who wanted someone to take her walking for an hour at a time. So it was decided I should take the job. Every Tuesday and Thursday after school I went to the lady's rooming house and walked with her on my arm for an hour. At times, I resented the job and even considered not saying, "A curb, one step." I wasn't always feeling kindly and didn't care if she tripped or not. But I never did carry out my evil thoughts. I always hoped that none of my friends would see me, but the fifteen cents an hour paid for my student activity book, and I felt a bit prosperous.

Herbert, who was now in the seventh grade, had made enough money running errands for a market to buy a book also. Though he usually covered himself with a brave front, he, too, was uncertain of himself. I knew it by the way he treated me when we were away from home. He ignored me. If we happened to walk home from school at the same time, he refused to walk with me. One day, in fact, we had left home at the same time and were discussing a game we had seen. A friend of his saw us and said "Hey, Herbie, who's your girlfriend?"

Herbert looked at me with disgust and yelled back, "Aw, she's not my girlfriend. She's just my sister." After that he was very careful to walk on the other side of the street if we left home at the same time.

Another way I knew Herbert was changing was that he often got in fights with other boys. He hadn't ever been much of a fighter, but now I expect he felt he had to prove himself. Then there was the fact that he and some of the other boys would sneak a cigarette once in awhile and smoke it. He tried a cigar once, but it made him sick. I don't know if Mama knew what made him sick, but she gave him some castor oil. That's punishment enough for anything. If you don't throw up before, you surely will after you swallow castor oil—it's terrible.

Herbert and I, at home, were the best of friends. We talked often about school and some of our mutual friends. We seldom shared with our parents. At our age, it seemed natural to choose up sides—the adults who never understood you or your friends who had the same problems you had. Of course, sometimes it became necessary to cross over from one camp to the other when pressures became too much to handle. This happened on one occasion which involved Herbert's math teacher. Herbert hadn't really changed sides, but the adults had.

The teacher, Mr. Roberts, was an understanding and helpful teacher when you were serious about studying. Though I hadn't gotten outstanding grades from him the year before, I'd had no trouble. Math was a deep mystery to me up to the seventh grade. I think Mr. Roberts considered students like me a real challenge. At any rate, by the end of the year I had progressed in my understanding more than anyone thought possible. My attitude, particularly, had changed. The mystery was gone. I considered it worthwhile to try to solve the problems, and often surprised even myself with my newfound ability. That was a milestone in my experience with arithmetic.

Some of the boys in class didn't share my difficulty in understanding but were openly rebellious about doing their assignments. This brought out in Mr. Roberts his worst fault—a hot temper. I saw him use a flat whipping board on some of the boys who were being extremely smart-alecky. We all knew they deserved it and no one really resented the treatment, not even the boys—for long, anyway.

Things were following somewhat the same pattern this year when Herbert was in Mr. Roberts' class. Herbert and some of the other boys had been asked to solve a problem on the blackboard. While standing there, the boys couldn't resist showing off and testing Mr. Roberts' temper. Everyone knew about the temper.

Herbert happened to be the closest when the lid blew off, and Mr. Roberts slapped him on the side of the face. Surprised and caught off balance, Herbert fell to the floor.

The kidding and joking were over. Herbert got up, brushed the chalk dust from his pants and completed the problem. The rest of the class session was very quiet. After school, word soon got around that Mr. Roberts had knocked Herbert Johnson down in the classroom.

I don't know how Daddy heard about the incident, but he did. Nothing is secret very long in a small town. I was told later that he visited the school board who had already heard the story. The next week, Mr. Roberts was gone and a substitute teacher took his place. Soon a new teacher had been hired to replace him and Mr. Roberts never taught again. He went into a small business for himself but stayed in town. I admired him for that but was rather sad that a person who was a born teacher had to give it up because of his temper. I know Herbert felt badly, too, and a little responsible.

Our sense of values were not always in line with those of our parents. We realized this at another time when our music teacher, Mr. Andrews, was fired for a fault similar to Mr. Roberts'. He was our only high-school music teacher and the band leader. I took a music appreciation class from him and enjoyed every class session. He was a particular fan of the "March King." We learned to recognize and name each of John Philip Sousa's stirring marches. I had never before been exposed to classical and semi-classical music. I found myself wanting to know more about some of the operas and the lives of a few of the composers.

Mr. Andrews had no bad habits that we knew about. Everyone liked him. No one ever mentioned that he had a temper, but one day it came out in such a manner as to shorten his teaching career at good, old Bentley High. He had asked the school board to provide a better record player for his music appreciation classes. The one we were using was squeaky and undependable. After several requests and reminders, the principal brought in an old player which someone had donated. Mr. Andrews took one look at it, picked it up and threw it out the second story window of the band room.

To all of us students that made Mr. Andrews some kind of a hero. When he was fired without benefit of a trial or without our being consulted, we had a cause. No one wanted to go to a school where they fired a man for doing what he had to do. What else could a man do when his request was granted in such a stupid way?

As always is the case, a leader of the masses came forward. One of the high-school boys gathered a group of friends around him, and together they planned the strategy for the entire school. The next day everyone was to stay home. Sit-down strikes were now in the nation. We were intrigued with the method and certain this was the way to handle our situation. We would stay out of school until Mr. Andrews was hired back as our instructor.

The strike wasn't as thoroughly planned as it could have been, of course, and failed miserably. That afternoon a special assembly of the entire school was called. No one considered staying away. The principal had a way with words and gave us a good talk on the inadvisability of having a sit-down strike. He promised the school board would do everything they could to iron out the problem with Mr. Andrews. At home, parents had heard of the plan for a strike and used their own means to avert it.

Mr. Andrews, also, did not come back to our school. He did get another job teaching music in a more understanding high school, which perhaps could afford a decent record player.

We learned a few things about collective bargaining: The strength is not in the numbers but in what you do with them. In our immaturity there was little organization.

As a collective group, we in junior high became our own entity. Our chief aim was to be with someone else our age, to be like everyone our age. As much as we were allowed to do so, we withdrew from the rest of society. While we were growing and learning, we wished that adults would leave us alone. They just didn't understand us. The real problem was that we didn't understand ourselves.

Though I still dreamed my impossible dreams, I began looking with more appreciation at the boys in my peer group. They didn't pay much attention to me and I was resigned to becoming an old maid anyway. It was too good to be true, then, when Mary Stater asked me over to her house one Saturday. She said her cousin, Harold, was going to be there. Even more wonderful, he was two years older than I, which practically made him a man of the world.

I thought Harold was the most handsome boy I had ever met and whispered that to Mary. She giggled and I giggled and he looked embarrassed. She told him my name and he said, "Hello, Bonnie May." We stood in front of the house for a few minutes while everyone tried to think of something to say.

Finally, Mary said, "Why don't we go inside?" And we did.

Harold said, "What grade are you in, Bonnie May?" Every word he said was beautiful and I knew I would always remember them. I was a bit embarrassed to let him know I was younger than he, but he didn't seem to mind.

Then he sat and cleaned his fingernails with his pocket knife. I thought even that was kind of special—that he carried a pocket knife.

I considered that men carry pocket knives for different reasons than little boys do. My brothers played Mumbly Peg or Root-the-Peg with theirs. Root-the-Peg was a disgusting game where the loser had to root the wooden peg out of the ground with his teeth. I was sure Harold would never have been so ungenteel.

I couldn't stay at Mary's for long because I had promised to go home and take the bread out of the oven. Mother had put it in before she went to check on a sick neighbor. She said that she might stay and see if there was some housework she could help with.

Harold said he had to leave, too, but planned to come back the next weekend and maybe he would see me then. Dare I hope he was coming back because of me? That was almost the same thing as a date which, of course, I wasn't allowed to have yet. So I wouldn't tell anyone at home about that part.

All week I could think of nothing except Harold, that I would see him again and that he surely wanted to see me too. I did recall every word he had said and thought of all the witty replies I should have made. He probably considered me one of the dumbest girls he had ever seen.

I asked Mary if she thought he liked me, and she said of course he did.

"Why? What did he say?" I plied her with many such questions but she didn't give me any actual remarks of his. I wasn't reassured. I said, "Don't you think he is good looking?"

She laughed. "No, I think his nose is too big." I tried to ignore the insulting observation because it was important that we keep our friendship alive. Mary was the only link between Harold and me.

When Saturday came, Mary told me that Harold would not be able to come over because he had to go to a track meet at his school, but she thought he would be there the next Saturday. So I waited another week.

The next Saturday afternoon, I went over to Mary's house wondering if I dared hope that Harold would be there. He was. Mary invited me in and Harold said, "Hello, Bonnie May. Glad you're here. I need someone to help me tie a necktie." He was dressed up and had a tie draped around his neck.

He grinned as he admitted that the tie belonged to his brother and he had never learned how to tie one. I hated myself for not knowing how either. For a moment, I teetered on the brink of not admitting my lack of knowledge and trying to tie it anyway. That way I could be close to him—at least until he discovered that I didn't know what I was doing. I concluded that it would be worse to try and fail than to admit I couldn't tie a necktie.

We talked about school for a few minutes and then Harold's older brother came by and the two boys left together. Mary said they were going to a movie with some friends.

That was the last time I saw Harold. Mary told me the next month that he had moved with his folks to another state. My first romance was dead before it was born. I couldn't help wondering if it would have been different if I had known how to tie a necktie. I comforted myself sometimes by saying, "Maybe his nose was too big, after all."

A few weeks later, Barbara Jean and I were visiting Grandmother Johnson. Barbara Jean volunteered us to gather the eggs from the henhouse. I couldn't understand that because she didn't like to work any better than I did. When we got to the henhouse, she set the basket down and said, "I wanted to show you something, Bonnie May." She reached into her sweater pocket and took out a single cigarette and two kitchen matches.

She explained, "I found this cigarette and I thought we could try it. I'll break it in two." I shook my head. I had been indoctrinated thoroughly on the evils of tobacco and was almost as afraid of that cigarette as I had been of the devil when I was a small child.

"No, thanks, Barbara Jean. I don't think I want to. You go ahead, though, and I'll watch and warn you if anyone comes."

She obviously was disappointed in me and bravely lighted the cigarette. She took a deep drag and coughed. She drew more cautiously and proudly blew out a puff of smoke. I was praying that God wouldn't strike her dead. I really liked Barbara Jean even though, at frequent intervals during our lives, I'd told myself I didn't. She soon scrunched the cigarette against a post and carefully put it back in her pocket, explaining she would finish it later.

We gathered the eggs and took them into the house. Then we went back outside to sit down on an old wagon wheel to talk. I was beginning to wonder at myself for believing that Barbara Jean might be punished for trying a cigarette. She looked all right to me and didn't seem to regret what she had done. I regretted having been such a coward. Would I always be afraid to try anything different? Was I destined to live on the sidelines all my life because I had so little courage? Where did courage end and good sense begin? I should be trying more things, experiencing more.

I didn't tell Barbara Jean what was on my mind. Instead, we talked about babies. She said, "You know, Bonnie May, we are old enough to have babies." I asked her how she knew we were. She said because we had hair growing under our arms. I said I didn't know if I liked getting old and she said yes, she felt that way too. The worst thing was all the responsibility. When you get old enough to have babies you have to be so careful.

She said, "I don't think you are even supposed to be hugging and kissing boys."

I thought, *Well, I haven't been doing much of that lately…or ever.* But somehow I thought I'd like to. All in all, it was a very depressing conversation and I was just as glad when we were called in for supper.

The next day was Monday and, at school, I forgot about the weekend. I was in a sewing class and proving to myself and everyone else that I was not meant to be a seamstress. Mother, who sewed so well, said that was all right; but she hoped I learned some of the simple things so I could at least use a thimble to do my own mending. Any time I could find a safety pin, I considered that a better way to mend than using a needle and thread. Monday, I spent the entire class time ripping out a seam I had put in wrong. One thing I was learning well: How to rip out seams.

After school, I saw Herbert and some of his friends going toward town. They always bought soda pop if any of them had money, so I thought that was what they would be doing. When supper time came and Herbert hadn't come home, Mother began to worry a little. She questioned me, but I couldn't tell her where he was. We sat down to supper without him. After the dishes were washed, we heard a knock at the front door.

Mother and Daddy rushed to the door and there was Herbert with three other boys holding him up. They said he had jumped up to grab a tree limb in the park and had struck his head, knocking himself out. He was conscious, but barely, it seemed. The boys left as quickly as they got Herbert through the door.

Daddy put Herbert to bed. Mama fixed some cold packs for his head. Herbert drifted in and out of consciousness all night. I think that Mother and Daddy were up most of the time changing the packs on his head. There was no bump or mark on his head, so they couldn't be sure what had happened. The boys hadn't been too explicit, and I didn't think they were telling the truth.

The next morning, Herbert began to talk sensibly and we still didn't find out any more. I understood his hesitancy to involve his friends. I told him what they had said and he agreed, "Yes, that is what happened." Further than that, we never knew if the boys were telling the truth or not. Even being a member of the society he was protecting didn't give me entrance into Herbert's confidence. He knew, of course, that sooner or later I would disclose everything he said. To all questions he simply replied, "I'm all right now. Just leave me alone."

Chapter Eight

Train Whistles in the Night

Many nights, after everyone else was asleep, I lay awake thinking about what I would like to be some day. I had read William Henley's *Invictus* and was certain that I, too, was the master of my fate and the captain of my soul. The train whistle on the night air said there were places to go and much to be seen. Countless exciting adventures were out there just waiting for me to have them.

In my imagination I would conjure up fellow adventurers, give them names and work out wonderful plots in which I always was the main performer. Romance, a home of my own and a family of my own entered into these fancies as did many other things—a good education, a name for myself, returning to see parents and friends at frequent intervals. I was ever loyal to our parents and could not bear to think of being away from them for long.

It was not always possible to know when I fell asleep because my fancies drifted right into my dreams, or so it seemed. They were so similar. Sometimes I felt guilty about longing for the future and was filled with fear that something of the present might be taken away. I particularly could not think of losing my parents or any of my brothers and sisters, so I always prayed for each of them by name before going to sleep.

One night I was awakened by a piercing scream. I knew it was my mother's voice. Soon, another scream even more terrifying than the first split the stillness of the night. The sound seemed to travel swiftly from our parents' upstairs bedroom outside to the woodshed in the back, bounce off and return to the house.

I listened, but no more screams—no sound of any kind except the breathing of my brothers in the next room. Sitting in bed I had disturbed Dora Lynne and Edna June, who both stirred slightly and turned over. There were no unusual sounds from upstairs and I told myself that, again, I'd had a nightmare. My dreams seemed quite real before, and I kept saying this had to be a dream also. I lay down, scooted under the covers and asked God to help me sleep. The prayer wasn't finished before I was asleep and it seemed that morning came a few minutes later.

The next morning, I heard Mother in the kitchen stirring up pancake batter for breakfast. She called and, one by one, nine children piled out of bed. Those of us who had to be at school the earliest were allowed to wash first. We also got served first at the table. Breakfast was one meal where we weren't all required to sit down together. We were required to wait until Daddy asked the blessing. He ate with the first bunch of us and prayed a blessing for all.

In the daylight and in the midst of the morning's usual activity came the assurance that last night's dream was nothing more than that—a bad dream. I didn't like talking about frightening things, nor did I like to look foolish, so was careful not to mention the dream to anyone.

The day was no different from most, and after school I had to stop at the library. I got home near supper time. Mother asked me to set the table and mash the potatoes. She was still folding some clothes she had just taken off the line. They smelled fresh from blowing in the outdoor air all afternoon. There was also the smell of fresh bread and clean scrubbed floors.

"Boy, Mother, you sure must have had a good day. You don't usually wash, bake and scrub floors all the same day." Mama smiled and replied "Well, I had all this energy. I even got a little mending done too."

After supper we sat around the kitchen table doing our homework. Mother took a book she was reading to her bedroom, explaining she was kind of tired from all that work and thought she might get ready for bed and read for a while. We all said, "Goodnight," without looking up from our books.

After I finished my homework, I got Billy Joe ready for bed and Daddy told Jimmy, Danny and Eddie they had better get in bed too. Allan Dale was allowed to stay up a little longer. He was still doing homework. I played a few games of "Tit-tat-toe" and Hangman with Dora Lynne and Edna June before we, too, decided to go to bed.

I dropped right off to sleep as soon as I curled up under the covers. The next thing I knew I was awakened by a scream. I sat up in bed, shaking all over. This was so real, but how could it be? The sound was exactly as I had heard it before. Then the second scream and, as before, it seemed to go out from my parents' bedroom window to the shed and bounce back. Now, however, there was activity upstairs. I could hear the sound of people walking. I heard my father's voice and there was someone else's voice—that of a neighbor. I couldn't distinguish the words.

At the same time, Dora Lynne sat up and said "Bonnie May, what is the matter?" Because I had to—older sisters begin to act like mothers—I told her nothing was wrong and for her to go back to sleep. I lay down beside her until I heard her breathing normally. I wondered if I should go upstairs. Of course, there would be another baby, but I had never heard my mother scream. I had never heard anyone scream in that way and I was frightened.

In a few minutes I heard a baby cry. The first cry of a baby is a most beautiful sound that even I could appreciate. I was thrilled, but also a bit apprehensive. I knew that the birth of a baby can sometimes take the life of a mother.

Before long, I heard Daddy coming softly down the stairs. He leaned over me and whispered, "Bonnie May, are you awake?" I wondered how he knew but nodded my head. He said, "You have a beautiful baby sister. She has soft curls. Do you want to see her?"

Of course I did. However, I almost hated my father for a brief moment. Why didn't he tell me about my mother? Hesitantly, I questioned, "Mama, is she all right?" He told me that she was doing very well, a little tired, but so happy with the new baby.

I slipped quietly out of bed and followed Daddy up the stairs. Mama lay in bed. She was very white, but she smiled at me and I knew she was truly happy. The doctor was washing his hands in a basin in the corner. The neighbor, Mrs. Jones, was just leaving. She had a bundle of clothes and rags under her arm. She told Daddy she would take the things home and wash them, and that she would be back tomorrow morning to help out after we left for school. She left and the doctor soon rolled down his shirt sleeves, put on his coat and, after shaking Daddy's hand, also left.

I looked at the baby who lay in a little basket that Mama had probably had ready but hidden from the children's many questions. Mama said, "How do you like the name Anne Louise?" Daddy said they wanted an old fashioned name for her. I agreed the name was beautiful and so was the baby. Actually, I thought she was the most beautiful baby I had ever seen. Her hair lay in dark ringlets which curled down around her ears. She was a delicate pink, not red, and just plump enough not to be wrinkled. I was certain that none of us had been so pretty. I would love helping take care of this live doll. It would be like having a baby of my own.

Mother and Daddy seemed pleased that I was so pleased. Daddy said we all must get some sleep now. Even Anne Louise. I went back to bed and soon was asleep dreaming about tiny babies. Sometimes it was a whole row of little dolls. Then one of them would move and she would be a real live baby—with curls.

After five consecutive baby boys we were all ready to spoil this baby girl. Even the boys considered her somewhat special—all but Billy Joe. He wasn't old enough to appreciate giving up his position of youngest to someone else.

In a large family, each child helps with the next one. Mothers seldom have to teach the youngsters how to tie their shoes, button shirts, tell time, eat with a fork or numerous other things. By observation and by prompting from an older sibling the younger learns. In our family, this system was taken for granted and a closeness emerged that might not develop in smaller families.

We often fought among ourselves, but were fiercely loyal if an outsider attacked one of our number. One day I heard Mother scolding Allan Dale for getting home from school so late. His face was dirty and a little tear-stained as he explained that there were some boys who had been waiting for him for the last three days over on Elm Street to beat up on him. Once they caught him, but he got away. The rest of the time, he had gone a roundabout way to get home.

When a boy is basically not a scrapper, the other boys sense it and the challenge is inevitable. That is the law of the jungle of childhood. Mother asked him if he wanted her to go to the teacher about it and he anxiously said, "Oh no, no. Don't do that."

Edna June had overheard the conversation, and I noticed the determined expression on her face as she slipped out of the room. Edna June, by nature, was a scrapper—boy or girl, it didn't matter; she loved a good fight. She seldom had to fight, though. She was strong and spunky and had enough sense not to antagonize anyone larger than she.

The next day after school, Allan Dale and another boy volunteered to clean the blackboards for the teacher; so he didn't leave school at the regular time. Edna June, how-

ever, did and must have run to Elm Street. She got there
ahead of the three boys who had teased Allan Dale and
she hid behind a bush. In a short while the boys came
along. They sat down under a tree, just waiting. When
they saw Allan Dale coming, one of them said, "Let's wait
until he gets closer so he can't get away. Then we'll beat
up on him."

As Allan approached, the boys stood bravely in their
three-against-one strength. Edna June, at the same time,
stepped out from behind the bushes. She must have made
a reputation for herself because the startled boys said,
"We're not fightin' her." They left quickly and Edna June
and Allan Dale walked home together.

Edna June said, "You probably could have licked them
all, but I wanted to be in on it if there was a fight."

After that, all of the boys in our family seemed to form
an unspoken pact that if anyone attacked one of them it
was an act of war against all. Of course, Herbert was too
old to take part in the maneuvers, but occasionally he
would amble up when a disagreement was brewing and
everything got peaceful very quickly. Word got around the
grade school that you'd better not pick on one of the
Johnsons or you'd have to fight them all. Strength in numbers is just one of the fringe benefits of being in a large
family.

On Saturday nights in Bentley all the stores stayed open
until nine o'clock. That was the big event of the week,
especially for the farmers who came to town to do their
weekly marketing. The young people from the farms usually liked to stand on the corners and talk or walk up and
down the whole three blocks of main street window shopping. Most of them stopped at the sweet shop for a coke
or ice cream before meeting their folks to go home.

The boys and girls who lived in town and could do the same thing any day after school took a very superior attitude. One Saturday evening, Herbert and I went with Daddy to the grocery store. In the car on the way, we commented to each other that there sure were a lot of "farmer hicks" in town tonight. We didn't know that Daddy was paying attention to our conversation, but if we had known we wouldn't have been prepared for the lecture we received.

Daddy had a great amount of respect for farm people. I think he respected and trusted all men more than most folks do. But having grown up on a farm, he could identify in a special way with farm boys and girls. He told us that calling anyone an unkind name always made us less of a person than they. It showed our lack of understanding—*ignorance*, I think he said—and was never necessary. He said there were many kinds of people in the world and we must be ready to meet them.

He wound up his sermonette with, "If you can't say something good about a person, don't say anything at all." As usual with Daddy's very rare lectures, what he said made sense and we grew a little that day in the area of accepting others.

That night after I went to bed and lay listening for the late train whistle, I wondered if people in far away places were really much different. Or was it just a matter of seeing what a person is and not what he appears to be? At this point in life I didn't even understand myself. How could I be expected to understand others? I was asleep before the train came through that night.

Being poor was a way of life, and most of the time we children didn't think much about it. I suppose Herbert and I realized more than the others that we were amongst the poorest. We were painfully aware of lack of money for movies, school activities and even some of the actual necessities.

I covered my awareness with a mask of pride and declared that if I didn't have it, I didn't really want it. Mother kept us so well dressed with made-over clothes that we usually looked like everyone else in school. I often wished she could do such wonders with shoes. In one box of cast-off clothing we had received, there was a pair of women's shoes which fit me. They were a bit old in style, a gray fabric pump with a little too much heel for girls my age. I chose to wear them, however, in preference to the government-relief shoes. It wasn't long before I regretted my choice. They were neither comfortable nor attractive, and I became extremely self-conscious wearing them. Determined not to miss school, however, I attended every day, going in to class early and shuffling papers at my desk after class to avoid leaving with my classmates.

During class, I sat with my feet tucked under the seat as far as I could manage. Those were not especially happy days. They did pass, though, for the shoes eventually wore out beyond putting them on again and I gladly discarded them for a comfortable pair of oxfords that Daddy had managed to buy. What price is pride!

As children everywhere do, we anticipated the holidays—Thanksgiving and Christmas. Not so much Thanksgiving; it was just a prelude to Christmas. Everyone began to get in a festive mood from Thanksgiving to Christmas. We looked for the first snow of the season, and, if we were fortunate, much good food.

On Thanksgiving Day in Bentley, our high-school football team played the last game of the season against their long-time rival, Belltown. The air was sharp and clear. Most of the students and many townspeople, bundled in warm wraps and blankets, attended the game. This was the exciting day the team had been preparing for all year.

Some families had their large Thanksgiving dinner after the game. We always had ours before the game because, holiday or not, we ate at six, twelve and six. Most of the time there were relatives who brought part of the dinner. There were always a few extra persons, without families, whom Mother invited. I remember an older lady we called Grandma Jacobs. She was nearly always at our table for Thanksgiving dinner. From time to time, Mother or Daddy added someone to the list and somehow we had enough food for everyone on that particular day.

Being one of the largest families in town and perhaps one of the poorest—though I didn't like to consider us so—we often were recipients of a Thanksgiving food basket from a church or service organization. I was human enough and hungry enough to enjoy the food, but proud enough to hate the humility of having the basket presented to us.

One day, when the folks were not at home and Herbert and I had been left to watch the children, I looked out the front window. A car had pulled up in front and two men were getting out. They unloaded a basket of food and started up our walk. As they knocked on the door, Herbert told me I had better answer it. I told him I didn't care if we ate beans for Thanksgiving, I was not going to the door.

I ran into the bedroom and closed the door. Herbert stomped to the door and accepted the basket, explaining that the folks were not at home. He thanked the men and closed the door. Then he called, "You can come out now, Bonnie May. They're gone." But he couldn't help adding,

"How silly can you get?" I didn't know, and neither did I know why it was so traumatic for me to acknowledge and accept the fact that we were poor and someone else might want to help. Instead of being grateful, I had an intense dislike for the faceless people who made up those baskets. I wondered if they really cared about the persons they gave them to, or if it just made them feel better the rest of the year because they had done this thing they thought was so great.

We started planning for Christmas soon after Thanksgiving. Herbert and I managed to save a little of the money we earned to buy a gift for our parents. We pooled our pennies to buy some small thing for each of the children. There were hair ribbons for Dora Lynne and Edna June, combs for each of the boys except Billy Joe—they were always losing theirs—a toy truck for Billy Joe and a tiny celluloid doll for little Anne. I saved twenty-five cents for a pocket knife for Herbert and hoped he would do as well for me.

At school we drew names and were told that the gifts should not cost over ten cents. Mama and Daddy gave us the money for these gifts and, all in all, it took four trips downtown to find just the right presents.

At church there was to be a Christmas program and all the children would participate. Two weeks before Christmas, we were given slips of paper with poems or scripture verses written on them. It was fun coaching the younger children, but I didn't like practicing for my part.

I knew I would be overcome, as usual, with stage fright. Sure enough, on the night of the program when I knew I was to be next, my heart started thumping so loudly I thought everyone could hear it. I was sure if I looked down

I could see it moving. My mouth became dry and I began to tremble. When I stood, my hands shook so badly I had to clasp them tightly behind my back. Then my knees shook. When I tried to speak, my voice shook, if it came out at all. As I had done so many times before, I vowed that I would never again stand in front of people and make such a fool of myself. Wild horses couldn't drag me up there.

Herbert was so calm it made me sick. Why did I have to have all the fear? After my part in the program was finished, I could relax and enjoy the rest of the program. The younger children seemed uninhibited and spoke so clearly and solemnly that I was genuinely proud of each of them. I wasn't such a bad coach. Several of the children were dressed in costumes and acted out the Christmas story. We all stood and sang: "Silent night, Holy night. All is calm, all is bright." I believed it was true but thought how wonderful it would be if just once I could be calm when performing before people.

Every evening at home we did some special thing. One evening we made vinegar taffy and everyone got in on the pulling until there were many twisted, silvery strands of the stuff. Mama was there with the scissors to cut the strands into bite size pieces before the taffy got too hard to manage.

The next evening, we made fudge and everyone took turns beating it until it was just right. The same evening we were able to make divinity and use the black walnut meats which represented many hours of work. Black walnut shells are very hard. We placed the nut on a flatiron and cracked it with a hammer. Several evenings and Saturdays had been occupied with our assembly-line, nut-cracking operation. We had two of the boys at a time cracking shells while others of us picked the stubborn nut meats out with ice picks. Someone had to double check to make sure no bits of shell were left with the nuts.

Inevitably there would be some shells left even after this careful inspection. The most difficult part of all was preventing anyone from eating the nuts prematurely. When we had filled a jar, Mother took over the guarding of it. It was only possible to make so much candy this year because Daddy had cut some wood for a neighbor and had gotten enough pay to buy extra sugar. Every year we made some candy for Christmas, but usually only one kind.

Another evening we had great fun shelling and popping corn to make popcorn balls. We had to police each other to keep from eating the popcorn while Mama cooked the syrup to make popcorn balls.

Trimming the tree was a family activity, also. Mama and Daddy had collected and saved a few ornaments, but the tree was mostly trimmed with strings of popcorn and cranberries and paper decorations which all of us worked on. The younger children delighted in pasting together the colored paper chains. Mama and I made flour paste for them by the buckets it seemed.

Of course, the basket of food episode was repeated. This time, however, Mama was home and thanked the donors in her usual gracious manner. Being poor had not robbed her of her dignity and she did not consider the baskets charity, just kindness. I liked giving to others, but really disliked receiving from others. I knew there had to be a better balance for me. Someday maybe I'd discover it.

On Christmas Eve, Herbert, Dora Lynne and I with some of our friends from church went Christmas caroling, calling on several elderly persons. We presented each of them with a small box of homemade candy. It made us feel so good to see their gratitude. They were surprised that someone had cared enough to come by on Christmas Eve. Some of them had no family. I couldn't even imagine holidays without a large family.

We stopped at the home of one of the carolers. Her mother had prepared large mugs of hot chocolate topped with marshmallows. This was beautiful, warm luxury.

We were home early and talked awhile with Mama and Daddy about the persons we had seen who had no family. After all the children except Herbert and I had gone to bed, Mama and Daddy brought out a box of gifts, a bag of oranges, a bag of mixed nuts and one of hard Christmas candy. Daddy's sister always tried to give each of us a small gift. Some years that was the only gift we received. But this time Herbert and I proudly got our gifts and slipped them under the Christmas tree.

We were allowed to help fill the Christmas stockings. I couldn't remember ever believing in Santa Claus and so there were no dreamy illusions to keep up. I enjoyed being a part of the preparations for the other children the most. Herbert was always a little grown up for his age and just didn't want to miss out on anything I got to do.

Each stocking got a fat orange first. Fresh fruit of any kind, except apples occasionally, was very scarce in Kansas in the winter. The oranges were a special treat on Christmas morning. Next came a handful of mixed nuts in the shells, then a handful of hard candies—the little round ones with a picture in the middle, or the spicy, ribbon kind. Herbert and I insisted on counting the pieces so no one got more than someone else. Next came a wrapped popcorn ball. Sometimes there would be a small gift on top of that when we were able to buy one. This time there were none, but we were sure that the gifts under the tree would more than make up for it.

We never had a fireplace so the stockings were arranged around the pot-bellied woodstove in the front room. The children, one by one, would rise very early, get their stocking and crawl back into bed until everyone else was stirring. Usually, the candy and oranges would have disappeared before breakfast.

After we had finished filling the stockings, Mama told us that we, too, must get into bed because everyone gets up so early on Christmas morning. We kissed her and Daddy goodnight and went to bed. I heard the train whistle that night just as my head was on the pillow. I went to sleep at once without taking time to think about Christmas in far away places. I was too much a part of this one to long for another somewhere else.

I was aroused by the sound of Mama's sewing machine. *It must be almost morning.* Puzzled, I slipped quietly out of bed and tiptoed toward the dining room where she sewed. Her back was to me and she didn't see me standing in the doorway. She finished a long seam and held up the garment to inspect it. I could see it was an outing flannel nightgown, just the right length for me.

I sensed that it was best not to be discovered and tiptoed back to my bedroom. I slid noiselessly into bed but lay awake for awhile thinking of the love I had just seen displayed. My mother, tired as I knew she had to be, staying up after everyone had gone to bed in order to have her gift for me finished, wrapped and under the tree on Christmas morning. It was more than just a new nightgown, which I needed, Mother was giving a part of herself. I glimpsed a little of the true meaning of Christmas. Could I ever love so well?

CHAPTER NINE

THINGS
THAT COUNT

The snow was slow in coming that winter and we were disappointed not to have it for Christmas. Seldom did we have such a sunny Christmas day. The boys went out in the afternoon in their shirt sleeves. Since they couldn't use the sled Daddy had made for the whole family, they would have to think of other ways to have fun.

The latest interest had been in making toy parachutes out of a square of cloth by tying the corners with string. They attached a small rock to the string ends, rolled the whole thing in a tight ball and threw it as high in the air as they could. Usually, it opened perfectly into a parachute and drifted gracefully to the ground.

I watched them for awhile and then went back into the house to read the book Herbert had given me for Christmas. I stopped on the porch to inspect the sled. Daddy was a proficient carpenter. He could build almost anything he had a mind to—if he could get the materials. His talents included: music, carpentry, painting, mechanical repairs and farming. He could even write poetry. Grandma once said he was a "jack of all trades, master of none." I think in a different time, under different circumstances, he could have been master of some also. He had made the sled of wood and painted it red. The runners were of hardwood but covered with a metal strip which would give a free glide in packed snow. I wished it would snow. We had a couple of old sleds and by doubling up some and taking turns the whole family could go sledding; all except Mother and Daddy, but once in a while they got into the fun also.

The snow, which didn't quite make it in time for Christmas, quietly arrived that night while we were sleeping. The next morning, Jimmy Lee awakened us by shouting excitedly, "Hey, there's snow! Come on, let's get the sleds out!"

I lazily opened one eye. Sure enough, there were little drifts of snow in the corners of the window. I tried to shush Jimmy Lee and persuade him to go back to bed for awhile. Getting up in the morning was not one of my favorite activities.

By this time, though, it was too late for more sleep. The household was beginning to stir. Mother was in the kitchen lighting the coal-oil stove. Soon I could smell the coffee. Next, the wonderful aroma of bacon drifted into the room. We didn't have this luxury often, but there had been two pounds of slab bacon in the Christmas basket.

One thing more enjoyable than staying in bed in the morning was getting up and having bacon and eggs.

Thankful for the flannel nightgown, I eased out of the warm bed into the cold room. My breath stood out in front of me to remind me of how cold it really was. I grabbed my clothes from the chair at the foot of the bed and ran into the kitchen in search of a warmer place to dress.

Mother looked up with her happy morning smile and said, "Good morning, did you sleep well?" She had a way of making each person who came into the room feel she was waiting for him or her alone. I don't know how she did it with so many depending on her.

I said, yes, it was really nice to curl up with the new nightgown wrapped around my feet all night. I could tell by her smile that she considered staying up all night to finish her Christmas gifts well worth the effort. I felt glad for her but a little guilty also.

I lifted the lid of the woodstove and put in a handful of corncobs from the basket. Then I poured some kerosene over them and dropped a lighted match in. Next, I dropped in some kindling and placed two sticks of hardwood on top of this. Soon there was a roaring blaze and I could enjoy sitting in the big rocker to get dressed. Only Herbert and I were allowed to start the fires. This wood range was large and we used it for most of the cooking in the winter. In the summer and when in a hurry, Mother would use the three-burner kerosene stove. She must have thought we would all be in a hurry for breakfast this morning. I expect she had seen the snow even before Jimmy Lee had.

The rest of the day was spent outside. Each of us was bundled up in heavy clothing, overshoes, mittens, scarves and stocking caps. Occasionally, someone would go in to dry out mittens or just to get warm. We took turns pulling the younger children on the sleds and went to a nearby hill and slid down it many times.

When we had tired of sledding, we made a snowman. Herbert helped Allan Dale and Jimmy Lee make a snow fort. They put Danny and Eddie to work stacking up piles of snowballs to use in a fight later. Billy Joe tried to help with the snowman, but we convinced him he was needed as errand boy to bring pieces of coal, sticks for the arms and an old hat for its head.

Winter may have been slow in coming but a long time staying. In the following weeks, there was more snow, harsh winds, sleet and ice storms. The thaw during the day was slight and only in spots where the sun shone the longest. The night freeze left many places slick as glass. For young people, sliding and skating on the ice was unending frolic. For older folks, stepping outside the door was a constant menace. They sprinkled salt and sand on porch steps to melt the ice.

Mother considered herself very fortunate, especially in winter, to have an electric washing machine, though we didn't have electricity. Our next door neighbors, the Carsons, had told Daddy that if he could get a washing machine, he could run an extension cord to their electric outlet. Daddy worked for a man who owned a second-hand store and was able to get a machine which needed some repairs. Of course, Daddy could repair anything mechanical and soon our mother was the proud owner of an electric washing machine. She heated large tubs of water on the woodstove. I enjoyed helping her with the wash, shaving in small slivers of the strong, brown homemade soap;

adding *bluing* to the second rinse; and carefully operating the wringer.

Hanging the clothes on the line in the freezing weather was pure torture for Mother and me. It is impossible to work the clothespins properly when wearing gloves, so we just stayed outside as long as we could. Then we came in and soaked our numb hands in cool water. The clothing froze stiff on the line in a few minutes. If the wind was blowing hard enough, the laundry would eventually dry even though frozen. If there was no wind, then just before supper we took the stiff garments down and brought them into the house to spread them around and finish drying. We always laughed at the bib overalls which could stand alone as though occupied by a headless ghost. Of course, they soon toppled over as they began to thaw.

One washday, while no one was watching, Jimmy Lee, the curious one, climbed up on a chair to investigate the washer. He turned a lever and touched the hard, revolving wringers. At once his fingers and his hand were caught and being rolled into the wringers. His screams attracted the attention of everyone in the house and nearby. Mrs. Carson could see through the window and rushed to the electric outlet. She pulled the cord just as Mother reached Jimmy and hit the release button on the top of the wringers. His arm was caught up to the elbow. As the wringers flew apart, Mother picked up Jimmy Lee and carried him to the sink in the kitchen. She poured cold water over his arm. Mrs. Carson came in and they thought it would be best to pack his arm in cold packs. I hurried outside to get a dishpan full of snow to make the packs.

No permanent damage was done, though Jimmy Lee's arm looked a bit bruised for days. Because there was no money to pay for it, we seldom called a doctor in those days. Home remedies were heavily relied on. Perhaps it was as Grandma said, "God takes care of little boys and big families who are poor." It did seem unusual that none of us ever had a broken bone and always seemed to respond to Mother's treatments.

Jimmy Lee was our most active member, the one who got into the most trouble, and the one who suffered the most when he was sick. I couldn't understand how children in the same family could be so different. Jimmy was particularly susceptible in the winter to *croup*. This was similar to asthma attacks. It was frightening to see him gasping for breath. Mother's favorite remedy for these attacks was to dip a long feather lightly in a few drops of kerosene. She would then touch the feather deep into his throat. The kerosene either broke up the congestion or caused him to gag and throw up. He didn't mind the temporary discomfort of the treatment, for anything is better than not being able to breath. He would soon be breathing normally and fall sound asleep.

Allowing us the use of their electricity for our washing machine was just one example of the Carson's good neighborliness. Mr. Carson was a barber. Every few weeks he brought his barber tools home, came over and told Mother and Daddy to line up the boys. Then he gave each a professional haircut, knowing full well there would be no money to pay him. Perhaps this was his way of showing gratitude for something Daddy did for him at times.

Mr. Carson was one of the friendliest, happiest men that we knew; but he had a problem which threatened to destroy him—he was an alcoholic. Most of the time he didn't touch alcohol in any form. Then, for some reason or other, he would have a drink and inevitably he couldn't stop. At those times, he stayed drunk for a week. Sometimes he didn't come home at all during that time. When he did, however, Mrs. Carson went to her sister's for a few days.

Daddy went over and helped his friend into bed. Mr. Carson was always remorseful and would talk a lot about how sorry he was that our boys had seen him and knew about his condition. Daddy was a good listener and stayed until Mr. Carson was asleep.

When Mr. Carson was recovered, he would shave and dress and go back to work, shaken and determined never again to touch a drop of liquor. And he didn't for several months. Mrs. Carson always came back and their household became normal again.

These fine neighbors enjoyed children so much that I think they would have loved having a family of their own. I wasn't told why they hadn't but wondered if it could be Mr. Carson's problem. They seemed to be happy together. Mother said that Mrs. Carson was Catholic and would never leave Mr. Carson for good. I think, even more than that, she loved him too much to leave.

Mrs. Carson's home was a haven to me. Though small and modest, it was spotless and orderly with cheerful touches here and there. There were fresh-cut flowers in a crystal vase, bright towels and potholders hanging in the kitchen, and matching dishes and glasses in the cupboards. It was very different from our home which was necessarily utilitarian. With so many children and so little money, there was no choice. I think our neighbor realized I was dreaming, as young girls do, of a home of my own; and that sometimes I became tired of little ones tagging at my heels. She often invited me to come over for a cup of tea. She would set out pretty dishes and make cinnamon toast. To me there was luxury in the fact that just two people could sit down quietly to talk over a cup of tea.

She talked with me as she would a friend. I told her about school events, assemblies, plays, pep rallies and how some of the girls dressed for them. She would show me patterns of clothes she was making and tell me about some new style she had seen in the department store. I was pleased to be able to talk with an older person in such a natural way. Actually, the Carsons were not old, but from my place in life they were. They had been married for six years. That seemed a very long time.

Mr. Carson was a good friend and enjoyed being with all of us children. I think he especially liked the boys. One day Daddy said, "We are going to take some eggs up to Grandma Loring's." At that time, she lived in a small town about forty miles away. "Would any of you children like to go along? We are taking the truck I borrowed because I must do some engine work on the car." That meant whoever went would be riding in the back of the truck. It seemed like fun. Then he added, "Roy Carson is also going because he wants to see a cousin of his who lives in Berryville."

When it was time to go, Mother and Daddy got in the front with Anne Louise on Mama's lap. They said that Billy Joe should sit between them on the seat. Mr. Carson said he would like riding in the back of the truck with some of us. Edna June had opted not to go. She and a school friend had plans, and she would be staying all night at the friend's house. The rest of us squeezed into the back of the truck. Mr. Carson sat in the middle, leaning against the cab.

On the way, Mr. Carson suggested we sing. We were surprised to find he knew all the hymns we knew from church. He had a good voice and led us in "The Old Rugged Cross," "What a Friend We Have in Jesus," "In the Sweet By and By," and others. The one we enjoyed the most was "Beulah Land." He didn't drag out the music the way most of the people in our little church did. He said, "Do you know 'When We All Get to Heaven?'" We knew some of it and he led us in a rousing finale to our trip. We were eager to go back home so we could sing some more. The singing on the way home was mostly a repeat of the trip there, but it was almost magical under the stars.

After I went to bed that night, I lay thinking about Mr. Carson and how enthusiastically he had sung the old familiar hymns. I was too young to understand the reason for his drinking problem or why he couldn't overcome it, but I thought he certainly seemed on familiar ground with the same God I knew. Was he going to be in heaven with the rest of us? I would just have to leave that all up to God who knew Mr. Carson better than I did. It was easy that night to thank God for good neighbors who were also good friends.

Though we would have these friends for many years, we weren't destined to be neighbors for long. Daddy rented a farmhouse three miles north of town. He said we wouldn't actually be farming, but the owner of the place wanted someone to live there to keep up the house and keep an eye on the barn and granaries. The rent was only $5.00 a month and the house was larger than any we had ever had. Daddy thought it would be very good for all of us to be in the country where there was more room to run, especially for the younger children. He said it would help give us a good sense of values. I glanced at Herbert and knew he was thinking, as I was, *Nobody better call us farmer hicks.*

I wasn't sure I liked moving to the country just as I would be starting to high school, but questioning Daddy's decisions was never one of our prerogatives—at least, not so anyone could hear. So we agreed, and so we moved.

It was a white, clapboard, two-story farmhouse with airy porches on two sides of it. The rooms were spacious and, at a time when I really needed to, I could actually have a little more space for myself. The bed in our room was large. The room was large enough for several bookcases and chests as soon as we could find them second hand.

The walk-in closet was larger than some of the bedrooms of former houses we had rented. We would still be sharing a double bed. One child per bed in those days was unthought of. Even if we could have afforded to buy another bed or two, there would not be enough blankets for them. Sheets were for rich people. In winter, each of our beds had a double-sheet blanket. In summer, it didn't matter anyway. Sometimes Mother saved flour sacks and, by sewing four of them together, could make a bottom sheet. When the weather got really hot and humid, we were always allowed to make pallets on the floor in whatever cool spot of the house we could find. This often created a challenging maze for our parents to get through when they got up first in the morning.

I liked this farmhouse from the moment we moved in. It was set back half a mile from the road. There was a well and large barn a short distance from the house. We would be carrying water up from the well. On windy days, the windmill did some of the work for us; but when there was no breeze, we had to do it all. Daddy taught us all right away how to unlatch the windmill shaft and attach the pump handle with a metal pin. Then we all practiced pumping. At first, it was fun; but naturally it soon became work, and Mother sometimes had to scold to keep the water bucket in the house filled.

Dora Lynne and I learned something else which we weren't sure we wanted to learn. That was the right way to scrub clothes on a washboard. With six boys who didn't care how dirty they got, this would turn into quite a chore. Probably the hardest part was carrying enough water from the well to fill the copper wash boiler. This large, oblong tub was used to heat the water on the wood range in the kitchen. When the water was hot, we transferred it to the wash tub set on two chairs. Another two chairs held the tub of rinse water. It was necessary to change the water in these tubs frequently, and so wash day became a major production line project.

I always volunteered to hang the clothes on the line. In good weather, that was a totally pleasant, soul-satisfying job. I sorted the pieces so that all towels were together, shirts hung together by their tails, dresses by skirt seams and overalls by their bibs. I loved to stand back and watch the wind take over as everything flapped in a merry, organized way.

Sometimes Dora Lynne would complain, "Bonnie May is just lazy. She always gets to hang the clothes on the line. She knows it's harder to scrub on the board." She was right, of course, but I didn't let her know I agreed. I took a turn at the board only when I couldn't get out of it. Mother did most of that anyway, but she insisted we learn how to do it.

I attempted to organize the boys for water carrying. They didn't take orders willingly, though. Their usual retort was, "You're not our boss when Mama is here. Go get the water yourself." But, when Mama was ready she gave everyone a responsibility and the grumbling stopped.

We soon had water in abundance in another form. We had a late spring rain. The farmers called it a gully washer, for it came down hard and didn't let up for a full day and night. A short distance west of the house, there was a gully about six-feet deep which was usually dry. The ground, still moist from heavy winter snows, couldn't cope with the heavy rain; so all the cricks, draws and gullies became full. Ours was frighteningly full.

The roaring water rushed its winding way down to a pond in the pasture two miles away. We asked Daddy what would happen if the rain didn't stop. He said we'd better pray that it stopped. The flood that might result from more rain could be devastating. We had a family prayer meeting—and the rain stopped. *Maybe it was going to stop anyway*. But, as Herbert concluded, "It's safest to have God on your side at a time like this."

Some people say that Kansas is a state of extremes. It's either too hot or too cold, too wet or too dry. Perhaps these extravagances in the elements caused us to appreciate more fully the beauty of spring and fall. As soon as the rain stopped, the sun shone and a very gentle breeze dried off the top of the ground so we could be outside again.

The boys had already investigated the miles of fields and pasture land around us. They were eager to resume their games of cowboys and Indians and early settler hunting. This was done with sling shots which Herbert had made for each of them. Each had found his own forked stick of wood which Herbert whittled and smoothed until it was shaped to suit him. Daddy had given them an old inner tube which they cut into strips with Mama's sewing scissors—much to her dismay when she found out. One eight-inch strip was tied securely over each of the fork ends. A small round of leather was required for the pocket to which the other ends of the rubber strips were tied.

The leather was the most difficult part of the sling shot to come by. We were ever alert for some old piece of leather that could be used. In that category were cast off purses, gloves, belts, straps and old shoes. The best and most supple was a shoe tongue. One tongue would make two pouches. By the time a pair of shoes was ready to be discarded, both tongues were gone. No one discussed where they went, however. Mother and Daddy most surely would not have approved.

With the boys and Edna June in the pasture on a hunting expedition, I noted that Mother and little Anne were taking an afternoon nap. Daddy had gone in to town to see about some work. The world seemed very quiet. I went into our bedroom to get my book of Kipling's poems. Dora Lynne was sprawled across the bed reading the Tom Sawyer book she had borrowed from a friend. She didn't even look up when I came into the room. I found my book and got a ragged old quilt from the closet. As I left the room, she had to question, "Where are you going with the quilt?" I told her I was going to read under my favorite tree.

South of the house a short distance, there was a grassy knoll with a large cottonwood tree. I had planned for a long time to sit under this tree and read, but hadn't before had the opportunity. I hoped the ground would be dry enough by now. It was and I spread the quilt on the ground so I could sit leaning against the tree. The sun was just warm enough. The soft, caressing breeze wasn't even related to the harsh winds that are so prevalent in Kansas. I wished I had brought another book. Kipling's robust and rollicking poetry didn't fit this moment. I was thinking about a beautiful poem by William Wordsworth entitled *Daffodils* which I had read at school. Now that would fit the day!

I lay back on the quilt and looked up into the tree. A bird's nest high in the branches seemed no worse for the storm we'd had. Could there be baby birds in it? Then I saw the mother bird fly up with a fat worm dangling from her beak. As she perched on the edge of the nest, I couldn't see her divide the meal, but was sure she had and soon she flew away for more provisions. Worms were easy to find after a rain.

I wondered how this little family could have survived the beating rain and wind with only tree branches and a nest for protection. The mother would have sat with her feathers ruffled out over the little brood and her head partially hidden under her wing. The design and building of her nest was an outstanding engineering feat. Her determined care and protection of the young was an inspiration. She would be just as determined when it came time to push the young out of the nest so they could learn to fly. How did she get all this knowledge?

I was reminded of a story I had heard about a hen house that had caught fire and burned down. A mother hen had stayed on her nest with her brood gathered under her wings. When folks began to dig around in the hot ashes, they saw the charred body of the mother hen. On pushing it over with a stick, they found all the baby chicks alive and peeping. It was a sad story—supposedly true—but it certainly illustrated the lengths any mother will go to protect her young.

Finally, I opened my book and read *Gunga Din* through again. I didn't want to waste all this wonderful solitude without doing some reading. Anyway, I enjoyed the sad feeling I had each time I read that poem.

That evening, after supper, we were all sitting around on the porch talking about what we had done that day. Mama was rocking Anne Louise in a big rocker. "Well," she said, "the baby and I had the best afternoon nap we have had in a long time. I feel so rested."

The boys discussed a rabbit they had tried to shoot with their sling shots. Of course, everyone had missed, but they were certain they would get him next time. He must have a burrow somewhere near where they had first seen him. Daddy asked if it were a cottontail or a jack rabbit. They thought it was a cottontail. He told them to be sure to bring it home for rabbit stew. There would be four rabbit's feet for the boys for good luck. "And don't forget to save the tail for a powder puff for Edna June." Edna June wrinkled her nose in distaste. She didn't know if she would want to powder her nose with a rabbit's tail. In fact, she didn't powder her nose with anything. Mama said the rabbit stew would be great.

Daddy asked Dora Lynne and me what we had been doing. Dora Lynne answered, "Reading."

She didn't ever waste words and Daddy knew that conversation wasn't going far. Once I asked her why she didn't talk more and she said, "When I have something to say, I'll say it." Without a doubt, she got into a lot less trouble than I because I so often said the wrong thing.

I couldn't just answer "reading," though. I told about the bird and nest and the little ones which I couldn't see but could hear them chirping. I told them I thought it was a miracle that the storm hadn't knocked down the nest or drowned the mother and her family. Before anyone could comment on this, I started talking about poetry and Rudyard Kipling. Herbert enjoyed poetry as much as I, so he was interested in the conversation. The rest of the children were bored with it and went around the house for one last game of Hide-and-seek before bedtime.

Daddy said that he had read some of Kipling's poems. I asked him if he read much poetry in school. He laughed, "We didn't only read it. We memorized it." Herbert wanted to know if he could remember anything that he had memorized. He said, yes, he thought he could still remember William Cullen Bryant's *Thanatopsis*. He proceeded to quote that lengthy poem, so far as I know, letter-perfect. At least, he didn't hesitate. We were amazed. This father of ours with only an eighth grade education was brilliant!

Our closest neighbor lived about a mile and a half down the road from us. This farmer, Mr. Collins, was one of the successful ones. He owned much fertile land with lots of granaries and more farm equipment than most who farmed in the thirties. The Collins family had one daughter who was away at college during the school year. Mrs. Collins called on us when we first moved in and asked us girls to come visit the next week when her daughter would be home.

Jean Collins proved to be an affable, unaffected girl who was as happy to have us for friends as we were to have her. She took us upstairs to show us her room. I didn't know whether to feel envy or sympathy. True, she had a beautiful, furnished bedroom all her own, but she was an only child. When we admired the large, four-poster bed, she said, "Yes, it was my grandmother's. It's really too large for one person." Then she added, somewhat wistfully, "I always wanted a sister." I felt ashamed of the times I had longed for a room of my own and not so many children around. It would be terrible to be all alone, even in a room this lovely.

Jean showed us her closet with rows and rows of pretty dresses. Edna June embarrassed me by remarking that they must have cost a lot of money. Jean said, "Not really. You see, I make all my own clothes. I love to sew." I noticed the sparkle in Edna June's eyes. She wanted so much to learn to sew.

Before we went downstairs, Jean looked at me thoughtfully. She said, "Bonnie May, would you be insulted if I gave you some of the things that I have outgrown? You are so nice and slender and I'm getting a little plump. Now, don't think I'll be hurt if you say no; but it is work to make a dress, and I'd love for you to have them."

I was surprised at my pleasure. For some reason, my strong false pride didn't kick in. She was so gracious. I was delighted. I assured her that I would enjoy having them if she was sure she couldn't use them any longer.

We had a beautiful friendship with Jean Collins which continued all summer. She asked us over for dinner sometimes. Some days we took Anne Louise with us and Jean would spread a large blanket on the grass in front of the house so we could sit and talk.

Jean told us about college. She was studying to be a teacher. I told her I thought I might like to be a teacher, but that was a long way off. I would only be starting high school in the fall. She said she felt that way once, but time really goes fast when you get in high school. Now she had finished her first year of college and was eager to complete the next three years. She might get a teaching job in our county so she could stay at home; but, if not, traveling might be fun. I had visions of traveling far, far away. But I knew I could never be away from our family for long.

Edna June said she didn't think she would like to teach school. She thought she might grow up and marry a rich man and not have to go to school anymore. She wanted to have lots of servants and live in a large house and travel all over the world. Jean smiled and said, "Well, you never know. You might just do that."

As usual, Dora Lynne just sat and looked wise, listening to the rest of us talk. When Jean asked her what she wanted to do, she said, "Get through school and go to college probably." Anne Louise crawled off the blanket and pulled up some crab grass shoots. I rescued her before she ate them. Jean said that was the cutest baby she had ever seen.

Mrs. Collins made our afternoon complete by arriving with a large tray filled with cookies, glasses and a pitcher of cold lemonade. She had chipped large chunks of ice to put in the lemonade. We ate, drank, and were extremely happy and content.

CHAPTER TEN

WE ARE ONE

None of us really missed living in town. As with most large families, we were a complete unit and, wherever we lived, managed to establish our own mini-kingdom. Activities were just different in the country.

Our cousins loved coming to visit. From three different families they came, each with their own lifestyle. Each family had fewer children than we had and, for the most part, their fathers had steady employment. No one compared wages as higher or lower in those days. The lucky ones were those who were working for wages. Any kind of work was a definite advantage. The Great Depression was in full swing.

If we considered the matter at all, we thought of Barbara Jean and Geneva as being the richest. Uncle Joe was with the civil service and someone said those were the most secure jobs. According to our standards of wealth, they always seemed to have everything—enough food, enough clothing. They never had to wear government-issue shoes, yet they came to visit our domain as often as they could.

Our kingdom was one of fun and frivolity. No one had time or the inclination to be bored. Any game could be organized in short order. Ingenuity was sometimes a necessity. If we wanted to play baseball and there was no baseball or bat, we made our own. Mother could take a ball of string or yarn, cover it with canvas or other heavy cloth, and stitch it up with a darning needle. The boys, often with Daddy's help, would find a board or tree branch, whittle a handle, and wrap it with cloth or tape….A baseball bat! The boys made stilts from scrap lumber. We organized races, tag games and dressing up the tall stilt men.

The kites we made flew as high as the string we had collected. One day when Barbara Jean and our aunt came out to bring some hand-me-down clothes, we were engrossed in a kite-making project. We had just pasted the paper on the frames when Aunt Corrie drove into our driveway. Quickly placing some rocks on the kites to hold them in place until the flour paste dried, we ran out to ask Barbara Jean if she could stay and fly kites with us a little later.

I could see she wanted to stay, but she hesitated, "Well, I can't run around much now. You see, I just went to the beauty parlor with Mama and we got our hair marcelled. She would be so mad if I messed it up. Hair appointments are rather expensive, you know." Sure enough, her hair lay in neat little waves all over her head, and she had on one of her better dresses. For a fleeting moment I was envious. I had never even been inside a beauty parlor. Envy soon turned to pity. Being rich certainly had its disadvantages. It's a lot more fun to be poor and be able to fly a kite whenever you like.

Aunt Corrie and our cousin didn't stay long. They had to get back to town to do some shopping. So we all waved as they left and then went to check the kites, put the tails on and get the balls of string ready. It was the first time this year we had made kites, so there was a good supply of string. We usually saved it all year, tied each piece securely to the piece before and added frequently to the ball. Mother kept the string ball in the kitchen for us to make our additions. The boys, however, preferred to save theirs wrapped on a smooth stick. That made it easy to unwind quickly when the air currents were lifting the kite quite rapidly. Kansas winds are often very strong.

Barbara Jean and Geneva were on Daddy's side of the family. On Mother's side there were two sets of cousins. Our cousin, Billy, had a younger brother and sister. Uncle Peter always had work. At first, he worked for the telephone company, maintaining and operating an office and switchboard in their living room. This was in a very small town. Later, he became unemployed temporarily and went to work on the W.P.A., the work program established by President Roosevelt to help the poor. My aunt sewed for people and took in ironing. So, while they were far from being rich, they weren't as poor as some during the Depression.

These cousins also liked visiting us on the farm. They sometimes wanted to stay all night, but usually got homesick before the night was over. It was hardly worth asking them to stay because we knew that cousin Jane, especially, would probably cry all night. We kept asking them anyway.

The other set of cousins were younger. Corbin was Jimmy Lee's age and his sister, Margaret, was just a baby. They lived on a farm and got along very well during the Depression. Farmers usually had enough to eat even if they didn't have much money to spend. It was different sometimes for the people who lived in town.

Corbin always thought it a great adventure to visit our family. He used to say, "When I grow up, I'm going to have ten children like Uncle Will and Aunt Mary." He was a good little sport and tagged along with any game we concocted. One afternoon that summer when he was staying overnight with us, Grandma Loring happened to be visiting us also. It was too hot to do much except sit on the porch and wish for cooler weather. That's what most of us were doing. The younger boys, however, had gone down to the barn. Mama was sitting in one of the rockers mending socks. Grandma was in the other rocker with a pan of peas in her lap. As she popped open the pods, she ran her thumb down inside the pod to loosen the tender green peas. These she dropped into a bowl on a stool beside the rocker.

Mother looked at the field of corn beside the house. She remarked, "Mr. Larson said we could use as much of that corn as we want for roasting ears when it is ready. That will be nice this fall!"

Just then the boys came up from the barn. Corbin's eyes were dancing with excitement. His hands were cupped shut and we knew he wanted to show us some treasure. He walked right up to Grandma and opened his hands slightly. Grandma, always a demonstrative person, shrieked, and several things happened seemingly simultaneously: Corbin, startled, dropped the half-grown toad he was harboring into the pan of peas; Grandma grabbed the toad by a hind leg, jumped up, spilling peas all over the porch, and slung the poor creature out into the corn field.

Corbin was crestfallen. He had not expected this reaction from his favorite grandmother. Allan Dale and Jimmy Lee were already in the field searching for the toad. Corbin was not far behind. Herbert and I were rolling on the porch with laughter. Grandma didn't think it was funny and told us to get up and help her pick up peas. Naturally, the boys didn't find the toad. Sometimes toads are smarter than little boys. Mother soon called everyone out of the field before they trampled down the corn stalks.

The boys spent the rest of the afternoon down at the barn looking for another toad. Mother sent Herbert to the well to pump a bucket of water. There hadn't been a hint of a breeze all day and so the windmill wasn't much help. I had to scrape potatoes, too small to peel, to cook with the new peas. Mama sliced and fried some salt pork. There were fresh, sliced tomatoes and a large bowl of leaf lettuce from the garden.

All of us liked wilted lettuce. We would cut several lettuce leaves up on our plate, pour hot bacon grease over it, sprinkle it with sugar and a few drops of vinegar. Last, we'd cut up a green onion on it. Yum! Good! When Daddy came home, just as we were getting the table set for supper, he brought in a 50-pound chunk of ice. There would be iced tea to round out our meal on this hot summer evening.

One of the games which the children liked to play almost proved a disaster. Several days after the toad incident, Mother and Daddy had gone to town for the day, leaving Herbert and me in charge of things. I had just put

Anne Louise to bed for an afternoon nap and come out onto the back porch to look for the rest of the children. Herbert was sitting on the step playing his harmonica. I unkindly told him he would wake up the baby if he didn't stop that screeching. He stopped playing and whatever he may have contemplated retorting was interrupted by a scream from the barn.

Eddie came running to the house yelling, "Danny's hurt. Come quick." Herbert, who could meet an emergency better than I, was quickly off the porch and running toward the barn. I followed very slowly, fear gripping me; my imagination, as usual, running ahead of my brain. I imagined a funeral and nine children trying not to cry. Mama and Daddy would be very brave.

Then I prayed, "No, God, please, we're supposed to be ten. That is an even number."

Just then Jimmy Lee ran out the barn door to meet me. I looked up and saw Herbert and Allan Dale helping Danny down the ladder that leads to the hay mow. Blood was streaming from one foot. Jimmy offered, "He ran the pitch fork right through his foot."

By this time, I was ready to be in charge again and began ordering everyone around. "Herbert and Allan Dale, help carry him to the house. Dora Lynne and Edna June, you girls get an extra bucket of water. Jimmy Lee, go out to the tool shed and bring in some turpentine." Then I ran to the house and put some water on the oil stove to heat.

When they brought Danny into the house, I had him sit on a chair and told them to roll up the pant leg above his knee and put his foot in the large pan I had set there. Then I poured some of the water that Dora Lynne and

Edna June had brought into the pan and began washing his foot and leg with some of Mama's lye soap. I sent Allan Dale to the closet to get the rag box and find a clean, white rag for a bandage.

After washing the foot thoroughly with the cold water, I washed it with the hot water and dried it, putting a clean, white rag underneath to keep the blood from the floor. I knew how this had happened. The children had been jumping from the barn rafters onto a pile of hay in the hay loft. Danny had landed on a pitch fork hidden in the hay and two tines had gone through his foot. Herbert said he had to pull pretty hard to get it out. I guessed that after all he'd been through, Danny could bear the next painful part of his treatment. I put a spoonful of sugar on top of each of the holes in his foot and poured turpentine through it. Daddy said the sugar cut the hurt. I don't know if it did or not. The turpentine was sure strong enough to kill the germs.

Allan Dale was standing by with the white rags which he had torn into narrow strips. He volunteered to do the bandaging. He seemed to have a natural talent for the job and produced such a neatly bandaged foot that we told him he should be a doctor. I think he liked the compliment.

Danny was the center of attention from then on. Mother and Daddy came home soon afterward, heard eight versions of the story and congratulated each of us for the way we had taken care of things. They thought it would be best this time to take Danny into town to the doctor because a tetanus shot might be needed. I don't think Danny was too happy with the prospect, but he didn't complain. After all, look at all that had already happened; and he was getting lots of attention.

When the folks and Danny returned, they told us the doctor said they were real lucky to have a family which took such good care of each other.

Another day, when the folks had to be gone for a few hours, I heard a car coming up the driveway. I looked out the window to see a shabbily dressed man getting out of his truck. I was afraid of so many things. I was fearful of strangers. I looked at Herbert. "Who do you suppose it is? What shall we do?"

If Herbert ever had any of the same cowardice I had, it didn't show. He said "Don't worry, I'll take care of it." He went to the door and, standing on tiptoe, reached above it for the rifle Daddy kept there.

I wasn't sure Herbert knew how to handle a gun, and I was as much afraid he might shoot someone as I was that a stranger might harm ten helpless children. I warned, "Be careful, Herbert." He opened the screen and stepped out onto the porch.

The man had come up a few steps, but when he saw the gun, he stopped. I heard him saying to Herbert, "Don't be afraid, son. I'm Mr. Larson. I own this farm. Is your father at home?"

Herbert stammered, "Well, no, not right now. I didn't know who you were and thought maybe—"

He was interrupted, "That's all right. Glad to see you are taking such good care of things around here."

Herbert set the gun inside the screen door and, standing on a stool, I quickly replaced it above the door. Herbert asked Mr. Larson if he wanted to come in and was told no, that he just wanted to tell us that the harvest crew would be coming into the upper north field of wheat next week and would be driving through our yard to get there. He said he would be back and talk with our folks about it in a day or two.

After Mr. Larson left, Herbert came in and I could see that he blamed me because he had met our landlord with a gun. He said rather sheepishly, "I'd never have thought of being scared if you hadn't been."

That made me kind of angry. I was beginning to develop a quick temper which didn't always endear me to those I really loved so much. I told him to shut up and leave me alone because how did I know it wasn't just some tramp? He retorted sarcastically, "Driving a nice truck?"

That made sense but I would never admit it. Making sure I had the last word, I ran upstairs calling over my shoulder, "He could have stolen it."

Herbert and I didn't stay mad at each other for very long. Our battles were usually verbal ones and neither of us spent much time pouting over what the other had said. Each of us concluded that we were right and patched up differences for a unity that was necessary to be the oldest and the "sometimes bosses" in our Johnson society.

The next week, when the combine and crew came through, all the children sat on the porch and stared. Allan Dale and Jimmy Lee came in the house to ask Mother if they could go to the field and watch the harvest. They were told they couldn't because the youngest ones would follow and get in the way. Also, Danny couldn't walk far yet with his sore foot. There wasn't any argument when our parents said "no." Daddy had always been very firm about that. So the boys went out by the tool shed to play a game of Mumbly peg.

Herbert was teaching Eddie David and Billy Joe how to play marbles. I was surprised at his patience as he drew the circle and then held his hand over each of theirs as he showed them how to shoot. Marbles were cheap in those days and most of the boys got a bag of them for Christmas. At school they played "for keeps," and some of the prettier *aggies* changed hands many times. A boy's status was measured by the number of marbles he owned. Each one zealously protected a favorite lucky shooter.

All very young boys hoarded initial collections in a small, cotton tobacco pouch. Mother sometimes made these pouches with drawstring tops from varied scraps of cloth. Usually, she used a plain flour or sugar sack and made several at a time. It was sissified to be seen carrying flowered marble pouches, so the material had to be plain.

The wheat yield that year was good. All the granaries were full. Mr. Larson stored some in a large bin on our place. This was a shed about a third the size of the barn and was covered mostly with tin. It had been a favorite hiding place during some of our Hide-and-seek games. Dora Lynne and I had avoided hiding there, however, because rats and mice also frequented it.

Harvest time and getting in the grain always meant the end of summer—and school just around the corner. That, of course, meant government books and government shoes for all.

I was actually anticipating going to high school. Herbert wasn't too happy with the idea of going to country school in the eighth grade. Especially after having attended seventh grade in town in the same building as the high school.

I was to stay in town during the week with a widow and her middle-aged bachelor son. I would go home on weekends. There wasn't any pay involved. I would get room and board in exchange for cooking supper and doing the supper dishes. The lady, Mrs. MacGregor, had rheumatism and couldn't get around very well. I had never stayed away from home for very long periods of time, but thought it might be rather nice to have a room of my own and some peace and quiet.

The first day at the MacGregor's I knew this wasn't what I wanted. Mrs. MacGregor was kind enough but she expected me to prepare the food her way. Right away, I discovered some new things about thrift. I was instructed to peel potatoes without water. Peeling the dry potatoes had the same effect on my nerves as hearing a piece of chalk screeching on a blackboard. Grandma Loring peeled potatoes dry, but hadn't insisted that I do it her way. Mother and I agreed that the potatoes should be placed in a pan of cold water. But I did it Mrs. MacGregor's way and knew I'd be unhappy about other things while there.

The next evidence of thrift appeared when I sliced a dried-up loaf of homemade bread. I was shown how to put the slices in the oven. I hadn't had much experience with stale food. At home, it took every bit of food we could get just to keep the family going from day to day. This bread even had a funny taste—not at all like our homemade bread.

After supper I washed the dishes and straightened the kitchen. Then I sat down with my schoolwork. The son, Cecil, went downtown. Mrs. MacGregor turned on the radio to hear the news. After the news, she asked me to get the paper for her and she read it. Mrs. MacGregor didn't talk much, but she made many distracting and disgusting sounds. She coughed, cleared her throat, got up and spit in the sink. Finally, I said I thought I'd go up to my room if she didn't have anything else for me to do. She said that was all right because she was going to bed soon anyway.

It was worse alone in the room I had been assigned. The silence was oppressive. I read a few more pages of history before turning to the math assignment. The word problems which never made sense to me only added to my depression. I opened my English book. This was easier for me and accomplishing the assignment cheered me somewhat. At last, I stacked all my books neatly on the big, oak dresser and started getting ready for bed.

The flannel nightgown would be too hot to wear, but it was all I had brought so I put it on anyway. I lay across the bed with my bare feet dangling over the side and looked up at the ceiling. Directly over the bed was a light cord with one light bulb. Fastened to the chain on this light was a piece of string looped over and tied to the head of the bed. I watched a lone fly walking up the light chain. I was glad to have his company. The string would be handy for turning out the light after getting into bed.

I thought about the kerosene lamp we girls had sitting on the dresser. It was always a contest to see who got into bed first. The last one in bed had to blow out the light. Every morning we were expected to bring all the lamps to the kitchen, fill them with kerosene, trim the wicks and wash the chimneys. If you didn't keep the wicks trimmed straight across, the lamp would smoke and get the chimney black. We had to spend extra time cleaning the chimneys when that happened. Each chimney must sparkle every evening.

I wondered if my sisters missed me. They were probably glad to have more room. Soon Anne Louise would be out of her crib and the folks planned to get another bed so she and Edna June would sleep together.

I heard the clock downstairs chime. I counted to eight. Was that all? At home only the two youngest would be in bed by this time. The rest of the children would be sitting around the big kitchen table doing homework. Daddy might be sitting on the porch playing his harmonica. Mother would surely be mending; or maybe she would have taken a lamp and a book to her bedroom. She loved to read in the evening when there weren't too many demands on her time. Or she might possibly be sitting in a rocker on the porch holding one of the children on her lap.

I wished I were home. This was a ghastly, quiet place. I allowed one or two self-pity tears. Then I remembered that Daddy had once said, "The worst you'll ever feel is when you are feeling sorry for yourself. If you can avoid that, you will be happy most of the time." I knew self-pity was selfish. I wondered if I could ignore it. I turned down the covers, pounded the pillow into the right shape and then lay down with only a sheet over me. It was luxury to sleep between two sheets. I'd pretend to be a fabulously rich girl. *Now, let's see, what shall I buy tomorrow with all this money I have? I am so wealthy. I am so-o-o miserable! I'm home-sick.* It is the worst sickness there is, I think. After while, I don't know when, I went to sleep.

On Wednesday, after school, Daddy came by to see how I was getting along. He said that he was starting on a job painting a house for a builder in town. I asked, "Will you be working every day?"

He replied, "Every day until the job is finished."

Then I employed my most effective and most unfair tool. I started to cry. "Daddy, I don't want to stay in town. I want to come home."

It was enough. My father was weak when it came to feminine tears. He also had a most vulnerable spot for any-

169

one who was homesick. When he was a boy and had to stay with his grandparents, he had experienced homesickness at its worst. He said that the attic loft where he slept was a frightening place for a little boy. He would crawl into bed holding the lighted candle high. He hated the thick dark when he blew out the candle. He could hear rats scampering and gnawing. He was afraid and he was lonely. He wanted to go home and he knew he couldn't. He couldn't even talk to anyone about his fears. In those days, boys were taught at an early age to be brave, never to cry and to always try to act like men no matter how much they felt like little boys.

I had learned about Daddy's regard for anyone suffering homesickness when I was much younger. When Herbert and I visited Grandma and Grandpa Loring for a week, we could always count on Daddy to come for us if we became homesick. Once, when our cousins, Billy and Jane, were staying overnight, Daddy heard Jane sobbing after she had gone to bed. We children didn't have much sympathy for her because we thought she could hold out for one night, at least. But Daddy got up, dressed, and rocked Jane and talked softly to her for awhile. Billy got up and decided he wanted to go home. Daddy helped them get their things together and took them home, twenty miles away. It was long after midnight when he returned home. I didn't hear him grumble or complain once.

Another time, a few summers before, I was visiting with Uncle Bob and Aunt Alice. They didn't have children and Aunt Alice asked all her nieces to visit every summer. That visit was fun for a few days. Two other nieces on Aunt Alice's side of the family were there; and we girls played games, sang songs, practiced putting on makeup and plucking our eyebrows. But somehow all the magic and fun of

170

being together wore off after the first week, and all I could think of was the brothers and sisters at home. I wondered if Mama and Daddy were all right. During the second week, I moped, complained and became generally obnoxious to everyone around. One evening, just after supper, I sat out in front of the house on an old tree stump. It was twilight and the children at home would be playing all their between-the-dark-and-the-daylight games. I thought about Longfellow's poem which I had memorized. I wanted to be home for the *children's* hour.

Soon I heard Aunt Alice calling me, "Bonnie May, come in here a minute." I wondered if she were going to scold me for sulking. Probably not. She didn't scold much. She was actually a very good person and I enjoyed being with her.

As I walked through the door, she said, "I just talked to your Daddy on the telephone and he is coming after you tonight. You'd better get your things together now." That was one of the happiest moments of my life. When you are homesick, you are sick all over. I felt well again.

Recalling all these things, I felt a little guilty that the same malady had struck me the first day in town. After all, I was supposed to start acting like an adult; but Daddy understood. He said that since he would be driving back and forth to town for a while he could take me to school and I could meet him at the job after school. I was relieved at the arrangement and agreed to finish the week with Mrs. MacGregor so that I wouldn't seem too rude.

That weekend, back with all the family, I didn't mind our crowded bedroom, or that Mama asked me to help with the ironing when I had planned to read, or when Herbert teased or anything else that happened. I was just so glad to be a part of our complete royal family again.

171

CHAPTER ELEVEN

A LOOK AT OTHERS

That winter, I am sure Mama wished many times that I had stayed with Mrs. MacGregor. Things went all right for us during the fall. Daddy had a job painting a house, and we were able to buy enough groceries to keep from starving. As the winter came on, there was no more work. A farmer was clearing a grove of trees, and Daddy spent several days helping him in exchange for wood for our winter's supply for heating and cooking. In our yard was a large pile of corn cobs which we depended on for kindling and a quick, hot fire in the cookstove.

Besides not having any money for food, I know it must have been a constant struggle for our folks to manage to get me to school. When Daddy couldn't buy gasoline for the car, he arranged with a neighbor to take me to town. Other times, I stayed for several days at a time with

Grandma Loring who, by this time, had moved back to Bentley. It was always a foregone conclusion that I would get to school somehow; that I would finish high school. I didn't even consider quitting.

We lived from day to day; meal to meal. I think Mother must have done a lot of praying that winter. She remained cheerful as though she were trusting something, or Someone, outside herself; which, of course, was just what she was doing.

When the last of the flour, potatoes or beans were used she seemed not apprehensive, but eager. Sure enough, the next day some provision would be made—usually from an unexpected source. Once, a friend sent a 100-pound sack of potatoes. That was all we had to eat for a week, but Mama knew many ways to prepare potatoes. One time, Daddy did a little repair work for someone who paid him with three fat hens. We ate one and kept two for a while for the eggs. It wasn't long before we had to eat the other two. Another time, Aunt Lottie, Daddy's unmarried sister, sent her tithe money to us. She said she thought that might be the best place the Lord could use it—at home, as well as in China or Africa.

Ordinarily, if we had any money to buy food, we bought large sacks of flour, a carton of canned milk and dry beans in bulk. I don't know what happened to the government allotments of food that year. We didn't have that assistance for most of the winter and I didn't ask why. Government shoes might be part of the package and my foolish pride told me anything was better than that.

Finally, a day arrived when there truly was nothing in the house to eat. I felt the responsibility more than I would at other times because Mother was sick. She'd had a miscarriage and was hemorrhaging badly. She stayed in bed most of the time. I got permission from the school to miss a week or so to take care of her and the children. I was given lessons to do at home. Daddy went out often to look for work, but there was none to be had.

With the two remaining cups of flour, I had stirred up pancakes and fed all the children breakfast. There was a can of evaporated milk left which I diluted with water and gave each of the children a small glass of it. For school lunches, I spread the pancake batter thin and was able to make enough for the children to have one cake rolled, with a little bacon grease, sprinkled lightly with sugar. At the country school they attended no one would make fun of them. No one had much and, in fact, most of the children shared with everyone else.

After everyone had left for school, I told Billy Joe to watch Ann Louise. She was beginning to walk and got into everything. He dumped a box of blocks in the middle of the floor to entertain her. I went out to the tool shed where Daddy was sharpening his saw. He looked up when I came in the door and I knew by his expression that he, too, was worried. We both believed in prayer, but I think we didn't have as much faith as Mama. "Daddy," I began, "I just used the last of the flour."

"I know," he replied, slowly laying down the small file he was using. "There is one thing we can do. It isn't much, but I talked to Mr. Larson about using some of the wheat in the granary. I told him I would pay him for it as soon as I could, but he said for us to go ahead and use as much as we needed and not to worry about paying."

I knew this must have hurt Daddy's pride a little, but he was truly grateful for the kindness. As one depression year piled on another, we hadn't lost our pride. We were forced at times to push it to the background and wait for better days. Everyone knew hard times would not last forever.

What a challenge! I began thinking of all the ways I could use the whole wheat. Daddy said he could grind some of it very fine to make flour. If we ground it coarsely it would serve for hot cereal. I could let some of that get cold, slice it thin and fry it for supper. There was some molasses left in the bucket. I would pour a little water in and swish it around to make more. We could pour that over the fried mush. Yum! Our supper that night was already provided.

For a long time we lived on Mr. Larson's wheat, prepared in so many ingenious ways I surprised even myself. When Grandma Johnson sent us a few cans of milk, some sugar and some eggs one day, I decided there might be enough ingredients to make a cake. So I concocted my own version of a whole-wheat-flour, sorghum-molasses cake. I was glad to find we still had a little baking powder. Then I discovered a tin with a few tablespoons of cocoa in it. It might be nice to have frosting for my unusual cake; so I stirred up a kind of pudding with milk, eggs, sugar and a little of the wheat flour for thickening. I dumped in a little of the cracked wheat. *Maybe the children would think it was walnuts.*

The cake didn't rise much and the end result, frosting and all, was not exactly phenomenal. Everyone ate some and the boys even asked for seconds—of course, they would eat anything. I thought it tasted like more of the same thing we had been eating for the last few weeks and wasn't sure I liked it chocolate-flavored. I could understand how the children of Israel felt when they ate manna for such a long time. I was determined, though, not to complain as they had. Mother always said, "What God has provided, we thank Him for. He knows what we need."

Mama didn't eat much in those days and I was sure it was because of her illness. I worried about that, too. I didn't know a great deal about recovering from a miscarriage, but I knew things were not right. Mama asked me to keep a fresh supply of clean rags on the table beside her bed. I rinsed and washed the soiled ones, hung them on the line in the sun to dry. I folded them neatly to be returned to the pile of clean ones. All of this when the children were at school, so they wouldn't ask innumerable questions I couldn't answer.

Mama hadn't gone to the hospital to have any of her ten children and no one thought it necessary for her to go now. Daddy talked to the doctor—to save the expense of a house call—and received instructions on how to elevate the foot of the bed, keep the patient very quiet and I don't know what else.

I didn't resent the work, even the distasteful washing, because I knew that my mother would far rather be doing it herself than have someone wait on her. I knew her condition was serious because she was so willing to stay in bed.

Mama's illness didn't diminish her faith. She still prayed daily for our food supply, the children's safety, work for Daddy and her soon recovery so that I could go back to school. As a family, we didn't often pray together and I didn't hear Mama pray these things; but she mentioned from time to time that I mustn't worry because she had "asked the Lord" for some particular favor. I knew she had, and I knew she would get what she asked for—eventually. I didn't like the way God took so long to answer some of the requests. Didn't He know I was getting behind in my schoolwork and ten children, a mother and father could just possibly starve?

But, of course, we didn't starve; and our mother began improving slowly. She was soon able to get up for a part of each day and, before I had time to indulge in much complaining to God, she was performing her household chores and I was back in school. The teachers were kind and understanding. They gave me the opportunity to make up any lessons I had missed. My grades weren't spectacular, but they were adequate. Possibly they were as good as they would have been if I would have had perfect attendance.

I had a natural tendency to slump in my studies after a class became routine. At the beginning of a school year—with a new notebook, a new textbook and a new subject to explore—I usually did extremely well. I'm sure most teachers had me pegged for an outstanding student. But as soon as the challenge of the new wore off, my grades dropped, I lost interest in the course and schoolwork was a drudgery the second semester.

The period of staying home had accomplished one thing for my character. It had caused me to see others with more compassion and understanding. I was concerned with my mother's feelings, as well as her health. I saw the struggle my father experienced to feed and care for all of us. I saw how very patient he was with each of us as we carried out individual responsibilities, and I saw how my brothers and sisters cared for one another. It was a healthy, growing experience of learning to look at others.

Jimmy Lee surprised all of us one Saturday afternoon with near heroism. Eddie came running into the house, calling frantically for someone to come see what Anne Louise was doing. I hurried out of the house with Dora Lynne and Edna June right behind, each slamming the screen door in succession. Eddie pointed to the windmill.

Our baby sister, who had been walking for only a few months, was climbing the ladder of the windmill. She had already reached a point about a third of the way up. I motioned for the others to be quiet so as not to frighten her and tried calling softly. The wheel was whirling in the strong wind. The pump was operating and the squeaking and clanging made it impossible for her to hear me. By this time, she had reached the halfway point.

I knew that I just couldn't hesitate any longer. Heights made me dizzy and we both might fall, but I had to go up after her. Before my decision could become action, however, Jimmy Lee came out of the barn to see what all the commotion was about. It took him less than a second to size up the situation and before anyone realized what had happened he was climbing the ladder.

I breathed a momentary sigh of relief. Jimmy was like a monkey when it came to climbing. I prayed he wouldn't have any trouble persuading her to come down with him. I think she was fascinated by the wheel and wanted to reach the platform around it. She hadn't learned the meaning of danger yet. With eleven flesh and blood guardian angels in attendance, she didn't have to be concerned with her own welfare.

Jimmy Lee reached her just three steps from the top. We held our breath as we watched him gently put an arm around her and, for a moment, they stood there as though he were talking to her. She put both arms around his neck and he began the descent. From that point on it wasn't any trick for Jimmy to get down. He needed only one hand to hold the ladder and he clutched Anne Louise with the other. Soon both were on the ground and all of us gathered around the hero and his charge. The rescuer enjoyed the attention, and the rescued laughed and chattered in a language no one understood. The next day, Daddy removed the four bottom rungs of the ladder so only taller people could climb it.

A few weeks later, Anne Louise frightened all of us with an even more serious incident. She was playing with some of her toys on the kitchen linoleum with no one paying much attention to her. A basket of cobs, some kindling and a pile of wood lay beside the range ready to build the fire for our evening meal. Beside all this was a cup of kerosene to be used over the cobs to start the fire more quickly.

Anne Louise got up from her toys and walked over to investigate the basket of cobs. No one saw her as she picked up the cup of kerosene and drank part of it. She gagged and Mama rushed over to pick her up. I saw Mama's face go white as she discovered what had happened. She ran outside calling Daddy and together they washed out Anne's mouth and gave her a few sips of water. They looked at the nearly empty tin cup. It was difficult to tell how much had been swallowed and how much had been spilled.

Mama wrapped Anne Louise in a blanket and she and Daddy took her in to town to the doctor. In a couple of hours they returned. Our sister was very pale, but alive. She was breathing in short gasps. Mama and Daddy took turns holding her all that evening. Finally, they insisted that all of us go to bed. I had made supper while they were gone. Everyone ate a little, but Mama just couldn't. She drank a cup of coffee when I brought it to her, but she wouldn't eat. I think she was identifying with Anne Louise.

All night Mama sat up in the big rocking chair in the kitchen holding Anne Louise. Most of the time the baby gasped for breath, but, as we learned later, at about 2:00 o'clock she began to breathe easily and normally. When we got up the next morning Daddy met us in the kitchen with a signal to be quiet.

He said Mama had been up all night with Anne Louise and that both of them had gone to bed a few minutes before. We questioned him and he said they felt that now our sister would be all right. She was breathing normally and sleeping. Mama's prayers had been answered again.

All of us were so relieved we had no trouble enjoying the pancakes Daddy had prepared. He loved to make "flapjacks," as he called them. When we asked him why he called them that, he would demonstrate how he could flip the skillet so the pancake would fly into the air and turn over, landing neatly on its other side in the skillet. We sometimes laughed and said maybe he should call them "flipjacks." He said, yes, and if he missed, he could call them "flopjacks."

The next week, when our cousins came out, Barbara Jean had a new camera which she wanted to use. We gave her our account of the windmill episode and she insisted on taking a picture of Anne Louise standing beside the windmill. Jimmy Lee really should have been in the picture, but he and Allan Dale were out in the pasture looking for Indian arrowheads. Friends from school had found some in their pasture and my brothers were certain they could also. Arrowheads were valuable for starting one's own collection or for their exchange value. Herbert once traded two for a pet duck—which he promptly traded for a compass. I think he sensed that even a pet duck might have a precarious future in our household.

When Barbara Jean left, she promised to give us one of the pictures of Anne Louise. Cameras were luxuries and we did not have one. I recalled that Mama had one a long time before, but it had been lost or perhaps sold. I didn't know, but it didn't matter. Even if we had a camera, we couldn't buy film for it so I thought it was good of Barbara Jean to offer one of the pictures.

I began to be grateful for the few luxuries that came my way. When you are very poor and you are very many, as we were, you don't think much about the things you can't have. You have each other and you have a lot of fun. At least, that was so with us. A sense of values naturally develops which revolves around the people you love and the things you do together.

On the periphery of this value system was my Grandmother Loring. I loved her and enjoyed being with her. The time spent in town staying overnight with her and my uncle were rather special times. My uncle, for several years, had worked as a meat cutter in a local market. Since Granddad had died and there was just Grandmother and Uncle Ed, they managed well enough financially. I don't think my uncle gave Grandma money. He felt if he provided for her that was enough. She told me once that he gave her a dollar a week to put in the church collection plate. My uncle liked having Herbert or me visit, but I suspected he didn't care for children in larger numbers.

So the others did not often spend time at Grandma's house. I didn't consider this unfair. Actually, I didn't consider it at all. There was always a warm welcome for me and I felt very much at home at Grandma's house. I was selfish enough to accept my position as my right.

At Grandma's, I had a bed all my own with *sheets*—that was sheer luxury—and I was allowed to stay in bed just a little later than usual. Grandma got up early to make biscuits for breakfast. As long as I can remember, Grandma always prepared homemade biscuits for breakfast. They were the best I had ever tasted anywhere. Grandma turned on the radio first thing when she got up in the morning. Before the local news broadcast, there was a recording of some kind. A girl with a lilting voice sang, "Let your troubles go bub-bub-bubbling down the drain." Perhaps it was a musical advertisement. I never discovered what they were selling, but it was a happy tune to wake one. I would stretch and yawn and, finally, when I smelled the bacon frying and the coffee brewing, I rolled out of bed and began to dress. I knew Grandma would soon be calling me and Uncle Ed to breakfast.

Wonderful as it was, I never stayed more than a few days at Grandma's house. The pull back home and the need to be with the rest of the children and Mama and Daddy was strong. I think Grandma liked having me because she enjoyed visiting with people. My uncle was a man of few words, just a grunt or nod of agreement now and then when Grandma talked. She needed someone who would say something back to her. She could count on me to do that.

Once, Grandma asked me to go with her to a friend's house. This was an elderly lady who lived alone and couldn't get out much. Grandma had baked some cookies and wanted to take them over to this friend. Right after supper, while it was still light, we walked the two blocks to the friend's house. We knocked on the door and heard her say, "Who is it?" Grandma told her and then we heard much shuffling and banging and clanging before she opened the door.

Inside, we were surprised to see a motley assortment of tubs, buckets, wash boilers, and pots and pans. The friend explained that, as she lived alone, she wanted to make sure no one got in without her knowing it in the middle of the night. She had rigged up a kind of booby trap which an intruder would have to knock down and move around before reaching her. She thought she could climb out her bedroom window by that time. My grandmother, who wasn't afraid of anything except snakes, lizards and creepy, crawly things, just smiled and said that sounded like a pretty good idea. I wondered what would happen if the intruder decided to come in the bedroom window, but I knew it wouldn't be wise to mention that.

My grandmother had many friends. She always had good neighbors because, as she said, "To have a good neighbor, you must be a good neighbor."

There were times when I wondered about some of her neighbors. Like the young lady who had so many male visitors. I heard her say, "I just have to have a man around. That's the way I am." I wasn't too wise in the ways of the world, so that went right over my head. Or the much older lady who went to our church, sometimes, called herself a Christian but used some mighty big swear words in her ordinary conversation. My grandmother, who was so intolerant of black people and Catholics, was able to accept almost everyone else. It was somewhat of a mystery to me. She was liked very much by her neighbors and so she must have been a good neighbor. Perhaps that was due to the fact that those she was prejudiced against didn't live next door. I didn't spend much time trying to understand my grandmother. I loved her and she loved me; I was comfortable with that.

Being at Grandma's house was so different from being at Mrs. MacGregor's. The situation was similar—a widow living with her bachelor son—but Grandma was *family*. That may have been part of the difference. More than that, Grandma and I understood one another and, of course, there was the bond of love between a grandmother and her granddaughter.

Many of the girls at school were wearing bright lipstick by this time. I had been told at church that it was a sin to wear lipstick. I tried to figure that one out. Why should it be a sin? With my brown eyes and dark hair I'd look better with lipstick, wouldn't I? I didn't want to risk being told at home that I couldn't wear it, so one day I spent a dime I had been saving for a very red lipstick. I hid it with a tiny mirror in a jacket pocket.

As soon as I was away from the family, I experimented. I didn't know whether to enjoy feeling wicked or to conclude that someone had made a mistake. There couldn't be anything wrong with this. I always wiped it off before I got home in the evening.

As all young people do, I was beginning to establish my own value system. Some of my decisions were valid and some, of course, were not. I remember wondering about a girl in my English class who had strong opinions on right and wrong. One day in the hall I was about to walk past a small group of students gathered around this girl, Marjorie Ecklund. At first I thought it was a friendly discussion, but heard her say quietly and evenly, "Let me out of here. I have to get to my next class."

The boys, four or five of them, were taunting her with, "Ah, let's see you get mad. 'Holy Joes' aren't supposed to, are they? Why don't you pray about it?" Everyone laughed.

I was never a very brave person. In fact, I considered myself rather cowardly, but a strong sense of justice forced me to stop and say, "Haven't you bullies got anything better to do?" The remark created just enough confusion to throw the boys off guard. Marjorie slipped through the circle and, together, we started walking down the hall. The boys didn't follow. I guess they were the real cowards in this scenario. Marjorie looked at me and smiled, "Thanks, Bonnie May. You're a real friend."

I asked her why the boys were teasing her and she told me that during a history test one of the boys who sat beside her had asked to see the answers on her paper and she had refused. After class she had explained to him that she was a Christian and that she had to answer to God for her actions. She didn't feel she should cheat on an exam or help anyone else to cheat. She had offered to help him study for the next test and he just laughed at her. To me, he was pretty stupid to turn down her offer. Her grades were usually straight A's.

I felt good inside. I had suspected this girl might be a "religious fanatic," but now she seemed like any other ordinary girlfriend. She didn't even mind identifying with someone wearing bright red lipstick. Startled at my own thoughts, I suddenly realized that she, too, was wearing lipstick. It was lighter than mine and complimented her gray eyes and fair complexion.

The incident put my value system in a little clearer perspective. I decided the really wrong thing I had done was the sneaky way I was using lipstick. I had just assumed what Mother and Daddy's reaction would be. Maybe I was wrong in my assumption, too.

After that, I was able to talk it over with Mother and Daddy and they said they didn't mind my wearing lipstick, but they wished I would do it in moderation. That seemed to be a favorite word of adults. I'd consider what that meant later. Even Grandma didn't think it was bad to wear lipstick and gave me a compact which someone had left at her house once. She said, "Put a little powder on your nose, too."

That year I suffered a beautiful, totally miserable, vicarious love affair. The girl in this affair was not me, but someone fabricated in my dreams and called by my name. The boy's name was Norman. He was real and I thought of him as a man. He was a senior in high school and I, a lowly freshman.

I first met Norman the summer before at a church meeting for children. It was not at our church. Norman's parents and two other families—related I think—had rented a small abandoned church building and held meetings there. They called themselves *Independents*, which was a new label to me. Mother said it just meant that they didn't belong to any particular church denomination. I liked the concept. The children's meetings were similar to vacation Bible school, and Herbert and I had gone because we heard they were giving free candy bars to everyone attending. They were. Other prizes were offered, also, for memorizing scripture verses, bringing others and attending regularly.

I brought the most children and won a Bible. It wasn't really a fair contest. I merely brought my brothers and sisters and a few of their friends. It was my first Bible. We had one at home which everyone could read, but none of us did that regularly, except Mama. Sometimes Daddy read aloud at our family devotions, called "family altar."

I was very proud of my new Bible with its brightly colored pictures and was determined to read it completely through. An old preacher we knew had read through the Bible seven times and we considered him extremely wise, but dull. The first part of Genesis was easy enough to read. I knew the story of the creation by heart, anyway, and skipped quickly over it. Further on, when I came to the "begets," my determination waned. They seemed even more dull than some of Brother Layton's sermons.

I wondered if Norman had read the Bible through. Maybe sometime I could ask him about it. At the end of the meetings a hay ride and weiner roast was planned for all the boys and girls who had attended. I looked forward to that day and hoped Norman would notice me. It wasn't to be, though. I was so busy taking care of brothers and sisters, threading wieners on a stick, rescuing a marshmallow about to fall, or watching to see that Billy Joe didn't stray too far away, that there was no time for being coy with Norman. Not that I had any idea how to be. He treated me exactly as he did all the other children.

That didn't stop me from dreaming. I considered this boy-man the handsomest person I had ever met. He was tall and strong and fair. His blonde hair had a way of falling in a wave over his forehead that seemed very romantic. His blue eyes twinkled with a bit of hidden mischief when he laughed.

All of my freshman year at school I hoped for an opportunity to talk to Norman alone. Several times a week I saw him, but it was always across the schoolyard, on the basketball court, filing with the other seniors into the auditorium for Friday assemblies or Thursday pep rallies. The freshmen and senior worlds were far apart.

I longed to be a senior, or at least a junior, so that our paths might occasionally cross. I was certain that it was meant to be and thought of all the "accidental" ways it might happen. I'd bump into him on the way to my locker, spill all my books, and when he stooped to help pick them up, our eyes would meet. At that moment, he would know, as I knew, that we were meant for each other.

I dreaded to see the school year end because there wouldn't even be the rare glimpses of Norman, and the possibilities of a wonderful meeting might be gone.

I spent a weekend with Aunt Alice and she made an appointment at the beauty parlor for me. It was rather frightening when I went in and sat under the machine with all those wires attached to my head. *What if they burnt me?* But they didn't, and I came home with my first permanent wave. Just as I had always wanted dimples, I had also always wanted curly hair. I was positively beautiful! Now, surely Norman would notice....He didn't. My notebooks had his name scribbled, written, printed all over them. I made sure that none of my family saw the name, though. I hated to be teased.

At home, I spent more time than usual lying around pretending to be reading a book or magazine. Each day I had a new imagery of Norman realizing suddenly that this girl he hadn't really noticed before was the only one for him. I thought of how it would be to have a date. I'd never had one. What would I do? Surely I would be poised and pretty and not appear to be easy to get. He would beg me not ever to go out with anyone else. I could imagine the two of us talking about our future, our plans for where to live, and how we'd both want a family of three boys and two girls.

The final assembly was Senior Recognition Day and all the seniors sat up front. Some of those receiving special recognition were seated on the platform with the school principal and our school superintendent. After we were seated, I was surprised to see that Norman was sitting on the platform right beside Mr. Albright, the principal. We stood, had a flag salute, sang the national anthem and then were seated. Mr. Albright and several other adults made some preliminary speeches and Norman was introduced as the class valedictorian—that meant he had gotten the highest grades. I had never considered him as a scholar. I knew he was an athlete. Now, he seemed more wonderful than ever.

After the assembly, as I hurried to my locker because I was to meet Daddy out front at 4:15, I saw Norman coming down the hall. But he wasn't alone. Beside him, looking up into his face in a disgustingly adoring way, was a senior girl I knew only as Ruth. Norman was smiling at her and didn't even see me. I wondered what he would think if he knew he had broken my heart and destroyed the dreams which he was so much a part of. At my locker, I tried to remember the combination for opening it. As I fumbled with the lock, I felt a light touch on my shoulder and heard someone say softly, "Bonnie May."

I turned to see Phil, a neighbor boy, standing there smiling shyly. I regained my composure and said, "Hi, Phil, how are you?"

Phil was a year older than I and he sometimes was allowed to drive the family car to school. As a matter of fact, I had ridden in to town with him several times. He explained that when he called home, his mother said my father had to go over to another farm on a job and for Phil to bring me home.

I thanked him and got my books, which he immediately offered to carry. I had always admired his manners. Now I looked at him and saw a fresh new acquaintance. I had never really looked at Phil before. He also had an escaping lock of hair that fell on his forehead, but it was black.

As Phil opened the car door for me, I felt laughter inside where the tears had been a few minutes before. I wanted to say that I thought life was very beautiful, but he wouldn't understand. Instead, I said, "Guess I was lucky you drove today, huh?"

CHAPTER TWELVE

THE ANGELS SANG

Summer was a welcome change of pace. The country school dismissed three weeks before the town schools. I think this custom had originated so that the boys could help their fathers with spring planting. As long as I could remember, I had envied the farm children who attended eight-month schools. Herbert and the rest of our family thought it was a fine idea. Next year Herbert would be going to town to high school with me.

Mother was feeling better now and didn't expect much help from us during the summer. We were to keep the lamps filled with kerosene and the chimneys cleaned, help hang out the wash, do supper dishes and watch the younger children. Dora Lynne, Edna June and I made quick work of our chores and were able to spend long hours reading, organizing games, going for long hikes and having picnics in the pasture or down by the creek. Anything would do for a picnic—basically it was homemade bread and whatever we had to put on it.

Food was always more plentiful in the summer because we usually had a garden with fresh leaf lettuce, green onions, radishes, peas, green beans, squash, carrots and small, new potatoes. Mama bought baby chick *culls* for a penny each. These were either very small and weak or had deformed wings or legs. With chicks, as with children, our mother successfully nursed them and made them grow. Thus, we were assured of many Sunday and special meals of fried chicken or chicken and dumplings. There would even be eggs in the fall until we had to eat the last of the chickens.

Daddy had some work in the late spring so we had a few weeks' supply of flour, sugar, canned milk and lard.

One chore which we girls hated and which had to be performed each day was *shooing* flies. The flies must have thought everyone was welcome in our home and they all came. There was always a child running in or out, holding the screen door open. Sometimes there was an open window which had no screen.

So once a day, usually just before supper, Mama closed the windows, called us in and stationed a girl in each corner of the room. We were provided with large dish towels which we waved vigorously. One of the younger boys stood outside the screen door waiting for Mama to tell him to open it. We waved the towels in wide circles, as wide and as high as we could reach, closing in our circle until we had almost reached the door. Then Mama would yell, "Open the door!" A swarm of flies was marshaled out the door and onto the porch. The entire process might be repeated several times until Mama was satisfied the last fly was gone.

Sometimes Daddy would spray with strong-smelling fly spray all around the porch and up under the eaves. Then woe to any unsuspecting child who held open the screen door or even was slow in entering so that a fly or two entered also. He was handed a fly swatter and must interrupt whatever else he had in mind to swat a prescribed number of flies.

Farms always have flies, and farmhomes with lots of children have lots of flies. At Grandma's house it was different. I especially remember Grandma Johnson's house and how fastidious our Aunt Lottie was. We felt she was too clean. All week, all of the house except the kitchen was closed, blinds pulled, to prevent dust from coming in. The kitchen screen door was always locked so that anyone wanting to enter must be let in by Aunt Lottie or Grandma. I don't think Grandma would have been so particular, but our aunt sort of bossed her around. When Grandfather was alive he was never allowed to come in without taking his shoes off first. I always thought it rather strange to see one old-maid aunt telling everyone what to do. But everyone did what she said.

As Mama said, though, Aunt Lottie was a good person—she worked hard to keep up the home, she helped in the garden and the yard, and she tithed her income. She must have made a little money from selling eggs.

When we were younger, Barbara Jean and I were probably a trial to this maiden aunt. For some reason, I was afraid of her. So I didn't do much except back up Barbara Jean who wasn't afraid of anyone, I thought.

One summer afternoon, when we were about ten years old, my cousin and I had been sitting under the peach tree in the back yard. We had made dolls of hollyhock blossoms and had given each of them a name and assigned them to a family unit. Soon, however, we became aware of the extreme heat and of how thirsty we were. So we jumped up and ran to the porch, banging on the door and making a great show of dying from thirst.

As Aunt Lottie let us in, she scolded, "Now, look what you have done. You let in four flies." She got two glasses of water for us and then handed Barbara Jean the fly swatter. "Now, be sure you kill four flies before you go back out to play."

Aunt Lottie went into another room and Barbara Jean began swatting flies. "One, two, three—there must be another one. Ah, I got two at once, and there is one on the window sill." She stopped swatting. "Bonnie May, I killed six flies. Open the door and let two more in." As I hesitated, Barbara Jean impatiently opened the door, allowing at least two more flies in. We both ran back out to resume our play under the peach tree. We felt very wicked and pleased with ourselves for what we had done.

Recalling the incident from a more grown-up perspective, I still thought it was rather wicked, but wondered why it made me feel so good at the time. Ah well, our values change.

I tried, at least on the surface, to live up to the values I had been taught. Sometimes I enjoyed going to church. At any rate, I felt God might not frown on me so much if I attended church. Most of the time the sermons were utterly wasted on me. I couldn't see how anyone could benefit from such long, dry, disconnected discourses. Our family, lined up on one complete row of pews, wiggled and squirmed and sought any means of diversion to pass the time.

Mama sat on one end of the row with Billy Joe and Anne Louise on either side of her. It kept her busy to keep them quiet. Herbert and I had a boy on either side of us. Herbert taught them how to make spitballs and paper arrows—which no one was to throw until church was over. I taught my charges to make paper boats from Sunday school lesson leaflets. Sometimes Edna June and Dora Lynne played Hangman or Tit-tat-toe on scraps of paper and, when Mama wasn't looking, wrote funny things in the hymnal. They called it funny. It was really rather dumb— like beginning on page one with a verse that said: *If you like this song, your nose is long. Turn to page 21.* And on page 21 they might write: *There's more you see. Ha-ha, hee-hee. Turn to page 33.* This could go on through the entire hymnal unless they were caught. It was always great fun to find a hymnal which someone had already inscribed.

I found myself wondering why I must go to church every Sunday. I believed in God, but didn't think He was doing much for me on Sunday mornings. One Sunday, a thought entered my mind, *I'll bet I could write a better sermon than this one.* There had been only two points made which I understood. In school, we had been taught to outline what we wrote and expound on the major theme without dragging it on interminably.

I entertained this thought for several weeks. *I might even write an interesting, entertaining sermon and mail it anonymously to the preacher. He could use it and everyone would be happier and I wouldn't even have to go to church.*

For some reason I couldn't explain, I was beginning to feel uncomfortable every time I attended church. It seemed I was making a show of worship which I didn't really feel. *I must be a hypocrite.* If I could only figure out some way of not going and still not feeling guilty. After all,

Daddy didn't attend often. He was nervous sitting still that long. We attributed his nerves to the war he had been in.

Mary's grandmother made me very angry one Sunday when she asked where Daddy was. I told her that he didn't feel well. She replied, "Well, the Lord may not feel like taking him to Heaven, either." I knew that kind of judgment was nearsighted and unfair. My father was a good man and a Christian. I knew this was a good Christian lady but she certainly had no right to judge my father.

Underneath, I knew I would never have the courage to write a sermon and mail it anonymously to the preacher. So in the fall, when our church had its annual revival meeting, the discomfort and unrest was still with me. On Friday evening, I went to the youth night meeting. There weren't any young people there except the few who attended church regularly. I allowed my mind to wander and didn't hear much of what the preacher said. Now and then, I was brought back to the present time and place when he shouted and pounded vigorously on the pulpit. I had missed his preceding remarks and, of course, missed the point. I wondered if the old pulpit could take so much pounding.

At the conclusion of the meeting there was an *altar call* as the congregation sang. I arbitrarily rejected much of what was being said, but when the altar call was given, I went forward with several others and knelt at the altar rail. I was overcome with guilt and confusion. Well-meaning women advised me to "pray through." First, I was instructed that I must "lay all on the altar." The phrase was explained—give up lipstick, nail polish, jewelry, short skirts, marriage if God so decreed. My stubborn soul refused. So much to give up. The issue was so clouded with negativism that I went home feeling miserable.

The next day I could bear the misery no longer. I was determined not to go back to that altar of my confusion, but knew I must have peace of mind. In my Bible I had read that when you pray you should go into your closet alone. In our upstairs bedroom in the old farmhouse there was a very large closet. I went in and closed the door. I fell to my knees and wept. I didn't know the right words, but I was sure they had nothing to do with lipstick and nail polish. I admitted my wretched condition and asked God to give me peace. It may not have been the prescribed prayer for sinners, but God accepted it and I know He accepted me!

As I opened the door of my heart to Him, Christ Jesus walked in and the floodgates of heaven opened simultaneously. That closet and my bedroom seemed flooded with light. My vocabulary had a new word and I could say only, "Glory, Glory, Glory!" I sensed that the angels in heaven were singing and rejoicing with me. I was a new baby born into God's wonderful family! True, I had been willful and had wanted no part of the "midwives" at the church altar, but God so graciously allowed me to be born anyway. I resolved that, from that day on, I would rely on the Bible for knowing God and not worry about fitting into any of the molds of man.

That evening, Mother, Grandma and I went to the final meeting of the week. The uneasy guilty feeling I'd had for so long was gone. As we sat down and opened our hymnals, I realized how much I loved everyone around me, even the ladies with long hair in buns and faces to match. Surely they ought to know that God isn't negative but, oh, so very positive. The God-imposed disciplines necessary for growth I was to learn later. For now, I was a happy child completely at peace with myself because I was at peace with God. What I had done was, in essence, what they had wanted me to do. I had submitted to God and asked Him to control my life.

At the close of the meeting another altar call was made. One of the ladies who had prayed so vehemently for me to "give up all" the night before started toward me. Mother, and how I loved her for it, interceded. I heard her say, "She's all right. She has been talking to God, herself." I wondered how she knew.

Monday, as I got ready for school, I had some misgivings. I was sure I was a different person, but didn't want anyone else to know it. Almost more than hellfire and damnation I dreaded being called a weird, religious fanatic. Some of the kids at school already called our little church the "holy rollers" because when the brothers and sisters got blessed, they shouted. One man sometimes got up out of his seat and actually skipped up and down the aisle. He was short and fat and funny; at least to the young people he was funny. We hid our faces behind a hymnal so we wouldn't get scolded for irreverence but couldn't control the snickers. I felt embarrassed for him.

This didn't change the fact that I was now right with God. What had happened was real but, for the moment, beyond my powers of expression. So I resolved just to keep quiet. *Maybe things would be the same at school and different at church.* There was still some confusion, but it didn't bother me so much anymore. I knew God would clear that up, too.

School wasn't too different from before. I must have been different because I found myself squirming when the boys swore or when someone told a dirty story. The pull to be part of the peer group was very strong, however; and instead of turning away from the stories, I sometimes added one of my own.

The only firm decision that I made was to read my Bible every day. Having already decided that I would not rely on what man said but on what God said, it was easy to accept scripture as God's infallible word. My trust in this source never faltered. So, religiously, every night just before going to bed I read one chapter of the Bible, beginning with Genesis. Admittedly, much of the reading was more routine than inspirational, but I was determined and, eventually, some passages began to take on meaning.

I liked being a sophomore in high school. We could now look with disdain on the lowly freshmen. As we had done the year before, they mostly ignored everyone except other freshmen. The sophomore boys traditionally initiated the freshmen boys. From year to year the rites were not highly original. On an appointed evening, the sophomores would kidnap six or eight of the freshmen boys, take them five miles out of town and dump them out to walk back to town in the dark.

I was afraid they might kidnap Herbert, and he was afraid they wouldn't. For some reason I couldn't understand, only the most popular were chosen for this initiation. The sophomore grapevine had received word that the initiation would be after the first football game. So it wasn't too surprising that Friday evening that Herbert didn't show up when Daddy came to pick us up after the game. Herbert had told me not to worry if he wasn't there and to tell Daddy that he would stay at Grandma's that night. I spilled the whole story to Daddy and he looked a little grim but started for home. He didn't say much as we drove along and I knew he was thinking over what I'd told him.

When I went upstairs to my bedroom, I heard Daddy downstairs talking with Mother. Then the screen door slammed as he went back outside and I soon heard the car going down the driveway. I wondered if he was going to find Herbert and give him a good lecture.

I dropped off to sleep and the next thing I knew was awakened by the sound of the car in the drive. In the dark, I looked out my bedroom window and saw Daddy and Herbert coming onto the porch. They weren't talking. I worried about that. They usually got along so well. I jumped back into bed and pretended to be asleep.

The next day, as soon as I could get Herbert alone, I questioned him. "What happened? Did Dad hit you, or lecture you, or what? What did the sophomores do?"

He gave me the look which he reserved for me and crazy people. "Bonnie May, you are really something. No, he didn't hit me and he didn't lecture me. Jimmy and Ted and I were taken out to five-corners, and they took our shoes." He seemed a little proud of that as he held up a dirty sock with large holes in the bottom. "I got to Grandma's house about midnight, and Dad was waiting there in the car in front of the house. He just said he didn't want me disturbing Grandma at that hour since she wasn't expecting me."

I shook my head. Well, Daddy certainly did have the patience of Job; and I knew that Herbert was happy. He was one of the selected few who would be a celebrity of the freshman class on Monday. *What a dumb tradition!*

The next month, we moved again. Mr. Larson was going to need our house for some newly married member of his family, so Daddy once more went house hunting. The place he rented was in the same school district, but closer to the river. The house was situated in a dense clump of trees.

I found it rather a charming place, with its weathered stone exterior and sturdy construction inside. Mother said she liked it because stone houses were cool in the summer and warm in the winter. At night I liked to stand in the back yard and become part of the splotches of moonlight filtering through the trees. It was possible to imagine I was in another land, completely surrounded by mysterious shapes and forms—some perhaps human and some not; all, however, seemed alive.

None of the rooms inside the house had been painted or wallpapered for many years and were streaked and sooty. Daddy immediately began to remedy this. In the large front room the wallpaper was not torn nor peeled. So Daddy purchased a supply of pink wallpaper cleaner. This was a spongy, clay-like substance which, when rolled and rubbed over the wall, did a remarkable job of restoring the paper to its original clean color. What a pleasant surprise to see the gray stripes and pink roses emerging!

The walls of some of the other rooms were not so well preserved, and it was necessary either to repaper or whitewash them. We ran out of money before all the rooms were completed, so the upstairs bedrooms had to be left until later.

One day, however, Daddy came home from town with the back seat of the car full of wallpaper rolls. How exciting to see so much new wallpaper! He brought them in and we began to open the rolls. No two rolls were alike. Mother asked why he had bought such a conglomeration, and he replied they were having a sale on remnants—five cents a roll. We agreed you couldn't beat the price, but what could you do with so many different designs and colors?

The bedroom shared by the four of us girls was to have been papered next. My imagination ran rampant. Why not use all of the designs? We could settle on a particular color range for each wall. Daddy, a rather finicky perfectionist, could not see using those partial patterns. No, he had a better idea: He would paste the patterned side and apply the paper on the wrong side. That way, we would have plain buff walls—neat and clean. He said we could add color by hanging up pictures and plaques. I was disappointed at having to give up the wild plan but knew it was no use arguing. When Daddy finished the room, it did look much better than before and gave us fresh incentive to keep it clean. Mama made some flowered curtains from flour sacks and hemmed half a sack to make a matching dresser scarf. Each of us girls had one drawer of the old scratched and battered dresser. Daddy promised that as soon as we got some more money, he would buy some paint for it.

I arranged my Bible, autograph book and diary on the dresser top, warning Anne Louise not to touch those things. I had a few other books, my lifetime collection, which I stacked neatly under the bed. Dora Lynne polished the chimney and base of our kerosene lamp and set it on one end of the dresser. Edna June had a tin thread box which she said could be our treasure chest. She instructed each of us to save a small part of any candy or cookies we might have and put it into the communal box. Then, sometimes at night after everyone was in bed, we could have a treat.

Though it wasn't necessary, she made us swear never to tell any of the boys about our treasures. Anne was not to be included in the secret, either.

I told Edna June I thought it would be more appropriate to use the box to keep our jewelry in. She laughed and said, "What jewelry?" She, alone, had a piece of jewelry— a ring with a blue-glass setting which had come in a box of cracker jacks.

I took cooking in school that year, thoroughly enjoying each class period. The first part of the year, we studied nutrition and discovered that there is a reason for the wide varieties of food. We learned what makes up a good basic diet. I knew that often our family lacked many of the daily requirements. At the end of the section on nutrition, our homemaking teacher asked each of us to do a study on our family's eating habits. We were to record each meal over the weekend, evaluate our findings and hand in the report on Monday.

For a long time I considered the possibilities. There didn't seem to be much point in making a report that said: *Breakfast—pancakes, Dinner—beans, and Supper—more beans or fried potatoes.* Finally, my pride and family loyalty won. I prepared a fictional study that met all possible standards. We had never eaten so well. I received an "A" on the paper. Surely the teacher must have known it was false, even though it did prove that I had learned the value of proper nutrition. My conscience wasn't so easy on me and I wondered what grade God would give me on the exercise.

The next section of the cooking class was almost all cooking. That year we learned the various methods of home canning. We were proud of the evenly packed jars of peaches, apricots, pears and apples. I don't know where the canned food went, but I assumed they used it in the cafeteria. Nothing was wasted in those days.

Next, we had a series of lessons on table settings and proper etiquette for various functions. We were allowed to plan a menu, purchase the supplies and prepare a festive breakfast. Several of the faculty were invited as guests and the girls acted as hostesses. The class was divided into groups so that this process was repeated three or four times. Our teacher was a very patient lady. She saw that we learned each lesson well.

Though she invoked a fierce loyalty in each member of the class, some teachers weren't so gifted. One day our beloved, soft-spoken Miss Thomas was absent. When we arrived at our assigned tables, we found the ingredients and a recipe for meatloaf. Everyone knew there would be a substitute teacher, but she hadn't arrived yet. That proved to be a mistake on her part. When most of the class was seated, a girl in the front row began making tiny balls of the hamburger in front of her. Suddenly, she turned around and threw a well-aimed ball at a friend in the back row. The friend, of course, retaliated. Someone in the crossfire joined the battle and soon hamburger balls were being thrown all over the room.

Not from any motive of goodness, I suspect, but because I am a coward or just couldn't stand to see so much food wasted, I stepped back and decided to stay out of the fracas. Several others joined me. We made up the cheering section, but became very quiet as we saw the substitute teacher step through the front door. We all knew her as someone who couldn't control a class, anyway. A huge dab of hamburger smacked her and disintegrated all over her face. Who can describe a room full of suppressed laughter? The harder we tried not to laugh, the harder we laughed.

That teacher was angry! She turned white, then purple with rage. She screamed, "Oh, you terrible, awful, terrible class." She turned and ran out of the room. We stopped laughing and began frenziedly cleaning up the mess. By the time the principal arrived, each girl was at her desk busily mixing and shaping a meatloaf. The great show of scholarly interest in the typewritten recipe was amazing. The conversation was at a bare minimum and then only for instructing one another on oven temperatures and time for baking. Mr. Albright looked a little puzzled, but merely announced that he was sending a monitor, a senior girl, in for the remainder of the period. As she had instructions to submit a list of names of any students who misbehaved, he trusted that each of us would conduct ourselves as adults. We did. Most of the meatloaves were probably not fit to be eaten, but we didn't mention that to anyone.

I felt a little sorry for the substitute teacher. Young people can be so cruel. We never saw this teacher again and I wondered if the escapade had so completely unnerved her as to end her teaching career.

The cooking classes, under Miss Thomas' careful supervision, planned and prepared the cafeteria lunches. Senior girls who took cooking were relieved of this responsibility the second semester because of the many senior activities. So the sophomore classes began their apprenticeship the second semester. This was probably the most practical and meaningful experience I had in cooking class.

We were assigned to rotating groups for menu planning, food purchasing, preparation and serving. This phase of the course taught us more than food preparation. It also gave us a real sense of responsibility and worth. In those depression days there wasn't much money to pay for extra help, and there wasn't much money for students to pay for lunches. The bookkeeping was another area in which we were being trained.

Although lunches were only twelve cents and the students received a well-balanced meal with dessert, the school cafeteria was self-supporting. At the end of each school year the graduating senior class balanced its books and had money left to buy some item for the kitchen. I think Miss Thomas must have been a remarkable person.

There was always a carry-over desire on my part to practice at home what I had learned at school. It was no use worrying when we didn't have well-balanced meals or even enough of what we did have to go around. The knowledge I had attained would always be with me. The genuine pleasure in preparing meals and attempting to serve them graciously was there.

Mealtime was the most pleasant time in our crowded household. Our parents required that everyone be washed and seated for meals. Each was to take some of what was served. There was no place for likes or dislikes. There wasn't enough food for finicky eaters. I don't remember ever hearing a brother or sister say, "I don't like that," about any of our food. Now, one of my cousins often whined about his food and his mama let him get away with it. We just didn't try it.

At our table, the conversation was expected to be pleasant. Complaints and arguments had to wait until later. Daddy said that when all the family sat down to the food God had provided, we shouldn't spoil our thankfulness with grumbling and quarreling.

I never felt underprivileged when there was plenty of homebaked bread. Even if we didn't have butter to put on it, it was still good. I read that bread was the staff of life and I think that must be so. We were all apparently quite healthy.

Because I had taken such an interest in cooking, I insisted on making all the bread. One Saturday, after I had made a large batch of bread, I was surveying the results of my labor and savoring the rich aroma of the warm loaves when the phone rang. It was two longs and a short—our ring. I answered it and Grandma Loring said, "Hello, what are you doing?"

I gave her a detailed list of the day's events: how Mama had washed in the morning, Anne had gotten lost but we found her under the porch, and that Daddy was painting at the Olsons. Then I added proudly, "And I baked bread today. Grandma, you should see those cinnamon rolls. I baked three dozen of them—I'll bring you some—and two pans of dinner rolls."

Grandma asked how many loaves of bread. I told her there were thirteen. I heard a gasp of surprise. "What did you say, Grandma?" She replied that she hadn't said anything and it must be someone listening in on our party line. We heard a click and knew she was right. Grandma asked to talk to Mother and I went outside where she was taking clothes from the line and told her Grandma was on the phone.

After supper, while it was still light outside, I went to our bedroom to read. Herbert came in and called up the stairs, "Bonnie May, come on out. We have company." I quickly tied my hair back with a hair ribbon and ran down the stairs. As I came out the screen door, I stopped short.

There I stood in a dirty, ragged dress, barefoot and hadn't even combed my hair. Why hadn't Herbert told me they were boys? I glared at him.

I recognized one of the boys as Carl Jensen, a boy in the junior class I had seen at school a few times. He introduced the other boy as his brother, Charles. Herbert said he and Charles already knew one another. They had some classes together at school.

Carl said, "We are neighbors. Did you know we live only a mile down the road?" I hadn't known because we always drove into town the other direction and they must have taken the winding river road to school. He added, "I guess we are on the same line, too. I didn't have much to do today and was listening in. All the neighbors do it sometimes. I just had to see who could make thirteen loaves of bread in one day." He grinned and I didn't know whether to be angry or glad. He didn't seem to notice how terrible I looked.

We all talked for a few minutes about school and then the Jensen boys said that they had to get back home but would be riding their horses the next afternoon. If we were going to be home they might come by and give us a ride. Dora Lynne and I had to admit we didn't know how to ride but would like to learn. Herbert had ridden some and assured them we would be home and looking for them the next day.

That evening before I went to sleep, I prayed a different prayer from my usual "Please do this and this and this." I said, "Thank you, Lord, for making me a woman." I would certainly try to be more presentable the next afternoon.

CHAPTER THIRTEEN

THE FIRST DATE

The horseback riding turned out to be a humbling experience, at least for Dora Lynne and me. We had spent more time getting ready for our neighbors' visit than we had getting ready for church that morning. After all, we went to church every Sunday. Having boys over was something that didn't happen often. We hurried away from the dinner table and cleared the dishes. Mother gave us special permission to stack the dishes and put the pans to soak if we promised to wash them later in time for supper. We promised and ran upstairs to make ourselves beautiful.

I took some oatmeal and mixed a paste which I smeared all over my face. I stuck my head out the window so the hot breeze could dry the "facial" more rapidly. Then I washed my face and rinsed it with cold water, patting it dry with a towel. Dora Lynne told me I should do this every day. It helped clear up the pimples and blackheads. I was especially aware of this particular plague of youth and felt no one in the world had a complexion as bad as mine. However, using the family breakfast oatmeal wasn't going to be my solution. I looked forward to the time when a dark tan would cover every imperfection.

Meanwhile, I looked in the mirror and saw very pink and very blotchy skin. I wanted to cry. Dora's generous application of the face powder which she had "borrowed" from Mother's dresser helped a little. Next, I put on some dark red lipstick and rubbed a little on both cheeks for rouge. Then we curled each other's hair with the hand curling iron that was heated in the lamp chimney. Dora Lynne was not so interested in getting her hair curled, but I told her that since one of the boys was about her age she should look pretty. When we finally were all ready and had changed into circular skirts and blouses, we stood back and surveyed each other. Yes, we really looked "cute." We ran downstairs to sit nonchalantly on the front porch.

Soon Carl and his brother came down the road, slapping their horses to a gallop and stirring up clouds of dust. They must have been trying to impress us. That was encouraging. We waved as they rode past our house and down to the corner, a quarter of a mile away. They turned and raced back to our gate. Carl was the winner. His horse could really go. Both boys slipped off their horses and tied them to the gate posts.

Dora Lynne and I got up and went to meet them. We stood under the big oak tree by the gate and talked for awhile about nothing important—the weather, the dust, the horses' names. Carl's horse was impatient to be moving. He didn't stand quietly as the other one did. He looked at me and I knew he didn't like me. I asked Carl how long he'd had the horse and he said about two years.

"Seems like a very nice horse," I lied.

Carl was obviously pleased. He was very proud of his possession. "Would you like to ride now?" he asked.

My romantic heart did a flip-flop. Of course, I would; at any rate, I thought I would. I thought I would be sitting up there behind Carl with an excuse to put both arms around him to hold on. "W-with you?" I stammered, and I could feel my face turning red. This time it wasn't from the oatmeal mask. Carl blushed a little, too.

He replied, "Well, no, you see Champ is kind of cantankerous about more than one person riding him at a time. But I'll help you up."

I had no choice. I was already committed—not only committed, but sentenced. So I swallowed hard, brushed my hair back and put one foot in the stirrup. Carl told me to hold the saddle horn as he helped boost my other foot over the saddle. It was awkward and embarrassing trying to sit on the circular skirt and tuck it modestly around my legs with both feet in the stirrups. The saddle felt slick and unstable to me. Carl said I would have to let go of the saddlehorn and hold the reins.

Meantime, Charles had helped Dora Lynne onto his kind, quiet horse, and she was slowly and gracefully riding down the middle of the road. *How did I ever get into this predicament?* Carl handed me the reins and off we went. That horse hated me and was out to prove it. We breezed past Dora Lynne; that is, the horse breezed—I bounced. I was more out of the saddle than in it. I never sat squarely in the saddle, but slid from side to side. I was desperate. I let go of the reins and grabbed the saddlehorn. I yelled, "Whoa!" and the horse went. On the fourth time up and down, I missed the saddle completely, kicked my feet out of the stirrups and fell in a sitting position in the middle of the road. Even that was a relief. Nothing was hurt but my dignity, and that was sorely wounded.

Dora Lynne's horse had become a little nervous and was picking up speed also. Dora Lynne, when she saw me sitting there, also fell off her horse. By this time, the Jensen boys were running to rescue us or, as I strongly suspected, their horses. Herbert and the rest of our brothers and sisters had come out to watch. It was great entertainment for them. Lined up by the fence, when they saw we could still move, they laughed more loudly and heartily than was necessary.

Charles said, "You know, old Champ won't let anybody but Carl ride him. We keep trying, but he keeps bucking everybody else off." I wondered why they had to try it on a coward like me.

As I brushed the dust off my skirt, I tried to save face by saying, "Well, I might have made it if I hadn't dropped the reins." Carl was kind enough to agree. But my mind was made up: No one would ever get me on that horse again, or maybe any horse.

Herbert asked Dora Lynne why she had fallen off her horse when she was doing so well. She said, "I saw Bonnie May fall off and thought I'd better too." It wasn't a very smart answer, but probably made as much sense as my excuse. For some reason, we always feel we have to say something in our own defense.

I saw Carl a lot after that—without his horse. I decided he might be a pretty nice person to know better. One evening, he walked down the road to our house and we stood out by the gate and talked for a long time. I stored his every word away in my mind's treasure chest to lay out and admire later on. He was a naturally quiet boy and didn't actually say a great deal. When he did talk, I managed to read volumes between the lines; and I talked enough for both of us. He was a good listener also, and that must have added to the intrigue. He seemed genuinely interested in what I had to say.

We were in the same shorthand class at school. I don't know why he was taking the class except that he planned to major in business administration in college and shorthand fascinated him. I also didn't know why I hadn't really noticed him before. Oh, I knew he was in the class, but he had been just another unimportant face. Now, suddenly, he had become a *very* important person. We sometimes exchanged notes written in shorthand. The notes didn't say much. His read: *Isn't it hot today? Won't you be glad when school is out?* Or: *Champ wasn't feeling too well this morning. I think he ate too many oats.*

Because it would be bad taste for me to appear forward, my notes were also not very exciting: *I may stay at my grandmother's house tonight.* Or: *Too bad about Champ. He is really a fine horse.*

Actually, I didn't care if he died. I probably didn't mean that; it was just one of those thoughts that occurs when you least expect it.

Carl had a silver identification bracelet engraved with his name. He gave it to me to wear; and that very evening, accompanied by an older brother, he came to our house and asked for it back. He was a little embarrassed, but said that his mother told him he had to get it back because it cost them a lot of money.

The next weekend, he showed me a pair of wooden bookends which he had made. They were decorated with carvings of cowboy boots. He explained it had been a woodshop project and that he wished he could give them to me, but he had already given them to his mother and she probably wouldn't like it much if he took them back.

I concluded his mother might be more trouble than his horse.

When Carl called to ask to take me to a movie, his mother and my mother had already talked it over. Apparently it was also Carl's first date and Mrs. Jensen wanted all the details worked out in advance. I told Carl I would ask my mother, and he said she had already consented. So, as casually as I could, I replied I would like to go and asked what movie was playing. I was sure that had already been checked out by his mother. He said it was one of Gene Autry's latest. He added proudly, "My horse, Champ, is named for his horse, you know." Even that bit of information didn't spoil my excitement.

My first date. For years I had dreamed of the occasion. Now, as the dream was about to become reality, I had some planning to do. There wasn't much time. This was Tuesday and the date was to be Saturday night. I told Carl goodbye and ran upstairs to decide what to wear.

That decision didn't take long. I had two dresses and two print skirts and blouses. One of the dresses would be suitable. It had been a hand-me-down from some of Aunt Corrie's friends. After Mama had finished fitting and making it over for me, no one would have known where it came from. I wouldn't feel self-conscious in the dress.

But I looked with dismay at my only pair of shoes. I wondered what it would be like to have more than one pair of shoes and never have run-down heels or worn-out soles. I would just have to polish the black oxfords and try to conceal the knots tied in the shoestrings. Then I remembered: The last time I looked there was no more black shoe polish; and, of course, there wouldn't be money enough to buy more before Saturday. Those shoes wouldn't look right anyway with the dress Mother had so carefully made over for me.

Later that evening, I complained to Mother that I was really going to look funny going barefoot on my first date. She laughed and said, "Now, honey, don't worry about it. The Lord knows all about your shoes. We'll just pray about it." I wished I had her faith. Since I didn't it was good to know that she, too, would be praying. I think I had faith in her faith.

The next day, at school, Carl handed me a note written in shorthand which read: *Are you still going to the show with me Saturday?* He blushed as I read it. I guess he was as self-conscious as I about doing something for the first time. I hadn't considered before that boys might have uncertain emotions. They always seemed so sure of themselves. I said, "Sure, I told you I would." He blushed again and I think I did, too. I hadn't meant to sound rude. Then we heard the first bell for the next class. I hurried to my math class and dropped into my seat just as the second bell rang.

It was hard to keep my mind on the problem being discussed. I kept thinking about Carl and the way he smiled. He wasn't exactly the answer to all my romantic dreams. He didn't talk much and when he did, it was about the farm or his horse. So far, he hadn't even paid me a compliment. That didn't really matter. He was a boy and I was a girl, and neither of us had ever been on a date before. I wondered what it would be like.

When Herbert and I arrived home from school, Mother was just finishing the mending. I noticed she had mended a small rip in the dress I intended to wear Saturday night. It was hanging, neatly pressed, on a hanger in the doorway. I disliked sewing and usually pinned all rips or tears until they became too large to do so, or I couldn't find another safety pin. I was glad she had taken care of the disagreeable task. Perhaps some day I would learn to mend, but only if I had to do so.

I thanked her for the mending. She said, "Oh, it doesn't take long if you just get started." And she added, "By the way, I know what you can wear for shoes." She went to her bedroom and came out with her good black pumps. She kept them for Sunday and they weren't badly worn even though she'd had them for several years.

She warned, "The heels may be a little higher than you have worn before, but I think you are old enough. You can practice walking in them before Saturday—don't want you falling down the stairs at the Grand Theater."

Yes, Mama's shoes would do. The style wasn't much different from those worn by the senior girls for dances. I thought about Mama's prayers and concluded she had helped the Lord a little this time. Maybe she was praying more earnestly for other things. I didn't know.

When Saturday came, I hurried through the morning chores so that I could wash my hair. I wanted it to be soft and shiny and just-right curly. That took awhile. I washed it with Ivory soap, rinsed it in clear water and then washed again with soap. Next, I used a vinegar rinse to make it squeaky clean and shiny. I dipped the comb in a sugar-water solution and set wide waves across the back. I rolled large, pin curls on the sides and ends. In order to dry more quickly, I sat outside in the sun for an hour.

I didn't even bother to read a book—just sat there on a stump, lazily squinting in the sun and dreaming young girl dreams. It was difficult to imagine what a first date would be like. Most all little girls have thought about it. As you get older, you place certain people and places in your dreams. Some of the girls at school had talked about going out with a boy, but I was never sure how much of what they said was true and how much was wishful thinking. Mama hadn't been much help other than seeing that I had the right clothes to wear. Our conversations about such matters were on a superficial level.

I wondered if Carl would hold my hand in the dark. He would probably buy popcorn for us. He loved popcorn. Up to this time, I'd never had a boyfriend and didn't know what to say if a boy offered to pay for refreshments. I'd led a very sheltered life.

Perhaps when we came home, we would sit in the car and talk for a while. He might even want a goodnight kiss, though I doubted it. But maybe he would. My older friend, Lauralee, said boys always kiss you goodnight after a date.

"Bonnie May," my reverie was interrupted as Mama stood in the kitchen door calling, "come peel the potatoes." I got up dutifully and went into the house to help get supper.

I hurried through supper and stacked the dishes, begging Dora to do them—just this once. I would take her turn the next time. "Sure," she said "for fifteen cents." I didn't have fifteen cents but promised her that the next time I earned some money I would pay her. She was very frugal and often used our I.O.U.s to her own advantage.

That evening, I would have gone in debt for much more than fifteen cents.

I slipped into the dress Mama had so carefully mended and pressed and looked in the cracked mirror on our bedroom door. I didn't have such a bad figure. A little skinny, perhaps, but with a little padding stuffed here and there I decided I didn't look so bad.

Would Carl like what he saw?, I wondered. I combed through my hair. For once, it seemed to fall just right with curls hanging down on my shoulders in a way that Lauralee said most boys like. *How did she get to be such an authority, anyway?* I had never really seen her with a boy. But, of course, she lived across town and I only saw her at church on Sundays, except when our two families got together.

Just as I brushed a little of Mama's face powder on my nose and applied a tiny bit of lipstick—I knew I would never get out the door with a lot of it—there was a knock at the door.

Carl was at the door when Mama opened it. She invited him in and he stood awkwardly waiting as I put on my coat. He was sort of dressed up in good pants, white shirt and a tie. He didn't have on a suit coat but was wearing a jacket which he didn't ordinarily wear to school. Must have been for dressier occasions. I didn't know how he dressed for church because his family belonged to the Methodist church.

Carl was probably as uncertain as I about first-date protocol because he stammered a bit as he bid my parents goodbye and didn't seem to know what to do with his hands. First, they were in his pockets and then he buttoned and unbuttoned his coat.

My big surprise awaited me as we got to the car: In the back seat sat his older brother. He must have seen my surprised look. He explained, "Mother doesn't allow us to go anywhere alone." There it was again. The specter of his mother making all his decisions. I was glad my mother wasn't quite that strict.

At the theater, his brother said, "Let's sit in the balcony. We can see better from up there." I hadn't been asked what I thought and was glad I hadn't. The whole thing was so new to me—having a date, going to the movies. In our family, we seldom had enough money even for Saturday afternoon matinees. When Carl went to get popcorn for all of us, I decided that we'd have a good time anyway. So I pretended to enjoy the cowboy adventures and tried to admire the famous horse. That seemed to be what Carl was most happy with—anything that had to do with horses.

Carl didn't hold my hand. In fact, he didn't pay much attention to me until the movie was over. Then he mostly talked about that *wonderful* horse. I wasn't sure I liked playing second fiddle to a horse.

There wasn't any nonsense after the movie. That Model-A Ford made a beeline to our house in the country. Carl did manage to walk me to the front door. He said "Good night, and thanks for going to the movies with me." That was it.

I went into the house thinking, *It doesn't matter what you dream, things are never what they seem; and sometimes the dream is better than the real thing.* But I hadn't given up. I still thought Carl was rather handsome and a very nice boy. Maybe the next time would be better, if there was a next time.

CHAPTER FOURTEEN

WHAT IS REALITY?

There were other dates—none so greatly anticipated as the first—and on each date the presence of a brother. Usually it was the younger brother, Charles. He was not dating anyone yet, so he invited Dora Lynne. She was glad to be included in all the activities, though she didn't seem to be especially fond of Charles or any other boy, for that matter.

I began wondering if my relationship with Carl was the real thing. Did I really want to be a farmer's wife? Did I really want to live in Bentley the rest of my life? It would be exciting, I thought, to go to some other state or country to live. I might even consider becoming a missionary. But I knew I couldn't live in a country where deadly snakes existed—never mind that we had rattlers in Kansas. We didn't often see live ones, anyway. And I knew I didn't like the idea of being boiled alive and eaten by cannibals.

Miss Cromwell, my shorthand and typing teacher, had talked to me about going to college. That would be great, but I knew that we would never be able to afford it. The folks would expect me to get a job when I graduated and help out with the family's expenses. I was becoming quite speedy with my shorthand, and accurate as a typist. There should be a job just waiting for my skills.

Carl came over one day and said that some of them were planning a hayride, and Dora Lynne and I were invited. His mother would supply the food for all of us. We thought that would be fun and planned for several days what to wear. As always, there wasn't really much choice for either of us. We each owned a school dress and a Sunday dress. I had a circular skirt and white cotton blouse that Mother had made from some hand-me-downs. Dora Lynne didn't actually concern herself much with what to wear. She was always so matter-of-fact about everything that she felt if she had one outfit, that was enough. I would have loved to own many glamorous gowns but knew that would have to wait until I became rich and famous, much later.

Meantime, I dreamed about the hayride. Now that would surely be romantic. Didn't couples usually ride together in the moonlight, holding hands and talking about their dreams? Carl hadn't shown much tendency to be romantic, but maybe this would be the time.

Dora Lynne and I were waiting in front of the house when the horses with the wagon of hay pulled up. We quickly hopped on the wagon. I had opted for the circular skirt and blouse, with the saddle oxfords and anklets I wore to school. After dabbing on a bit of lipstick and tying a pink ribbon in my hair, I had decided that I looked rather cute. Carl, however, didn't seem to notice. He said, "Hi," and motioned for me to sit down on a pile of hay. He was driving the team and his brother was on the wagon seat beside him. Well, so much for a romantic ride.

After going a few miles on the country road, we came to a meadow where preparations had been made for a large bonfire. Carl looked down at me and said, "Will you help carry the wieners and marshmallows while I start the fire?"

And we really did have fun around the fire, roasting wieners and marshmallows. I especially enjoyed roasting a marshmallow, pulling off the crusty part and roasting what was left. Some of the kids could do that three times before the marshmallow was used up.

More than the food, though, I enjoyed the sunset. The sky had turned many shades of pink, purple and orange. We could see it through a maze of trees—cottonwood and spruce. I sat thinking, *There has to be a poem about this sunset.*

Right then, I decided that what I really wanted to be was a poet. I loved reading Browning, Keats and Shelley. The Brownings had such a beautiful love for one another and Elizabeth wrote such poignant poetry about it. My brother, Herbert, and I would sit for hours reading poetry to each other. Perhaps I'd be a poet and leave a legacy for all the world someday. On the way home, riding with my back against a bale of hay, I started mentally composing a poem about the beautiful sunset I'd experienced:

> The sun gone down has left a haze
> of glowing pinks and blues,
> An indistinct but glowing maze
> Of cottonwood and spruce.
> Sunset in all its glory,

> Beauty of the highest degree,
> Thrills my heart and fills my soul
> With endless rhapsody.

Well, it might never win a literary award, but I was pleased with my effort. I was sure I could become a poet with a little more practice.

The country school my younger brothers and sisters attended served as a community meeting place for all kinds of events. The school was located a mile from our home and the students could easily walk to and from school. Some who lived further away would ride a pony to school. Of course, they were the envy of all who didn't have a pony, but they were always friendly enough to give the smaller children turns riding the pony.

The country schoolteacher often lived with a local family. Usually she had grown up on a farm and was already accustomed to that lifestyle. She was expected to build a fire in the woodstove after arriving at the school. She could then appoint some of the older boys to keep the fire going during the day. It was not an easy life, but most teachers—ours as well—were quite flexible.

She often had all eight grades in a one-room school and had to juggle the schedule so that she could spend some time with each grade level individually. It seemed to work. Farm young people coming into town to begin high school did very well scholastically. I think part of the reason the system worked so well was that all country schoolteachers were very dedicated to their profession. Seeing progress in their pupils was more important than the rather meager monthly pay, even more important than any inconvenience of having to do all the "housework" around the school.

People living within a ten-mile radius of the school would meet once a month in the evening just for a pot-luck and evening of visiting, catching up on all the news and local-talent entertainment. Sometimes it would be group singing; other times anyone who played an instrument or sang solos was called on to perform. Also, one very popular form of entertainment was when someone would give a reading—usually memorized. Some of the readings were funny and some of them were very sad, but always they were presented with a great deal of expression.

One day, Carl sent me a note in shorthand class saying the meeting was to be next Thursday night and we'd better all come. He and his brothers were going to play their musical instruments—a trumpet, a violin and an accordion. They would also be singing several songs. I was more than glad to return a note saying we'd surely be there. And we were—our entire family, including little Anne.

Whole families came together and there were always small babies and toddlers as well as grandmothers and grandfathers. After the initial welcome by Carl's father—he was on the school board—the entertainment began. One of the local farmers who fancied himself a comedian, told an assortment of jokes and stories about his neighbors. Everyone laughed. Then Carl and his brothers got up and played several numbers. Carl and his older brother, Clement, sang "Red River Valley."

After the entertainment, tables were set up around the edges of the room and the food was spread out. There was a bountiful amount of fried chicken, potato salad and baked beans. Also, it seemed every woman in the area had baked a pie. For some unknown reason, I had never liked desserts but ate my share of fried chicken and potato salad.

My mother had made a large container of baked beans and they were delicious—everyone said so.

The evening ended with hearty handshakes and goodbyes. Carl just said, "See you at school tomorrow." Another fun, but not so romantic, evening. I began to wonder if there would ever be more to our friendship than the surface relationship we seemed to have. I decided women were just more romantically inclined than men.

Daddy came home from town one day and said he thought we should move back to town. He had found a house to rent, and there wasn't much point in living in the country and having to spend money for gasoline to drive back and forth. Herbert and I were both in high school, and Daddy was getting a few jobs painting and wall papering; so we started packing. Mother and I were quite adept at wrapping dishes in newspapers and putting them in boxes. Daddy borrowed a truck from a friend and we made several trips to our "new" home with all our belongings.

There was a little discussion, bordering on arguing, amongst all of us concerning who would sleep where. There were four bedrooms. Mother and Daddy, of course, would have one of those, leaving three for ten children. The six boys would get two bedrooms and we four girls would have to share one. Daddy managed to get another bed, so there would only be two of us for each bed.

In the past, we girls had often slept three in a bed. Someone was always kicking me in the back. Even though no one liked to sleep in the middle, I usually had my say about that. I was the oldest and considered myself the boss and authority in such matters. Mother and Daddy allowed that.

For this house, Daddy had found a large, old dresser that we girls could use. We divided up the drawers and arranged our few belongings as we each saw fit. I insisted on using the top, though, to set Carl's high school picture and a scrapbook he had given me. There really wasn't much to put on top anyway.

After finally settling in our new home, we all went back out to the farm to sweep the floors and make sure we hadn't left anything behind. I looked in every corner and went into the back yard to search for the senior pin I had lost. Most of the kids had bought senior rings, but the pins were cheaper and I had managed to save enough to buy one.

I was finishing my junior year at high school when the senior rings had been purchased. I was so proud of the little gold pin which had the letters B-H-S on it. I couldn't understand how I could be so careless as to lose it, but it was never found. That was just another lesson in deciding what was real and what was truly important in life—it certainly wasn't material possessions. Our family was a close-knit group, an entity in itself, and we were happy. What we had or didn't have in material possessions was not what made us happy, having each other did.

One Saturday night I got permission to use our car to drive my sisters and two girlfriends to town, just a few blocks away. On the way, someone said, "Let's go to Aurora. There is a wedding dance there tonight." The French settlement was well known for its wedding dances. Whenever anyone married, the whole community got together and provided a festive dance with refreshments. Everyone was invited.

I shook my head and said, "No, I already asked Mother if I could go and she said, 'Absolutely not.'" Both Mother and Daddy knew how to say "no" quite firmly without any further explanation or argument. I really never thought about openly disobeying.

Edna June, usually the most adventurous, remarked, "Oh, I don't think we need to go to the dance, but let's just drive over there. Mama didn't say we couldn't do that and, anyway, there's nothing to do here. This whole town is pretty dead tonight."

Everyone quickly agreed with Edna June and we started on the road to Aurora. It was perhaps twenty miles away. I had never been there and wasn't sure of the distance.

We drove for five or six miles when I began to feel extremely guilty. I did not like to disobey my parents, and I knew that rationalizing as we had done was the same as disobedience. I turned the car around, to a flood of protests.

"Bonnie May, what are you doing?"

"We aren't really disobeying—just going for a little ride."

"Come on, don't be such a spoilsport."

I tried to think of my own face-saving argument. "Well, I just remembered something that I have to do. I've got to get back home." Of course, that wasn't true, but I just didn't feel up to answering them with what would amount to a sermon. My character hadn't developed to that point yet.

We had no sooner turned around and started back toward Bentley when the car motor sputtered and died. Now I remembered: Daddy had said before we left home, "There isn't much gas in the car. If you can get twenty-five cents together among all of you, you can drive around town a little." We were out of gas and five miles from home on a dark, country road that was not traveled enough for us to be certain of anyone helping us—not before morning, at least.

"Now what do we do?" Edna June asked. I remembered she was the one who had gotten us into this pickle in the first place.

I had an answer for her; for all of us: "We get out and push." No one was very excited at the prospect but everyone got out, anyway. We didn't want to sleep out there. Going downhill wasn't too hard, especially for me. Since I was the only one who could drive, I got in and did the steering. I would then get out and, holding the front door open and one hand on the steering wheel, help push uphill. Ever so often we had to stop and rest until we all got our breath; then repeat the uphill, downhill business.

Fortunately, most of the road was level and we finally saw the welcome lights of Bentley in the distance. After one last rest stop, we managed to push the car into town. There was a gas station and we pooled our change. Fifteen-cents worth of gas, but it got us home. We didn't talk about the escapade around the folks. We had learned our lesson, I felt, and that was that.

The school year was almost over and our junior-senior prom was being planned. Mother said she had some material to make me a formal. I wasn't sure I wanted to attend—Carl had said he didn't plan to go—but when my friend, Mary Ann, and I were asked to help with the table decorations, we began to get excited with the thought of going.

We decided to go together. There would be a dinner first and then a program, and after that a dance. Neither of us danced but wanted to see the festivities. The dress Mother made was pink organdy and rather pretty. The shoes I had weren't exactly right for a formal, so Mother told me I could wear her high heel pumps I had borrowed for my first date with Carl. All in all, I felt properly dressed.

The evening was festive. The gymnasium was decorated with colored streamers of crepe paper and the tables with flower and candle centerpieces. We girls had helped set the tables and were rather proud of the overall effect. The lights were lowered and only the stage had spotlights. Our table was occupied by other girls who didn't have dates. Somehow, it didn't seem to matter much then.

After the meal, there were some musical numbers. One of the senior girls with a beautiful voice sang a solo. Next, there was a violin solo. Our high school music director led in some group singing.

Then the band began to gather on the platform in readiness for the dance to follow. Mary Ann and I decided we would go home as soon as the first dance started. Mary Ann's mother was waiting for us in the parking lot and she offered to take me home on the way. It was a pleasant evening but certainly not one dreams are made of. I was beginning to find that reality was not always the fulfillment of dreams.

First and foremost in my mind was the matter of finishing high school. There was just one more year to go and I was determined not to let anything interfere with getting that diploma. It was humiliating at times not to have the right clothes for every event, especially shoes. I *did* dream about that. Someday, I would own many pairs of shoes. With all the clothes I intended to have, I would have a pair of shoes to match every outfit. But, for now, I took pride in the fact that our family had such great times together without material things. However, I knew I spent too much time indulging in daydreams about clothes. I wasn't very proud of that.

From the standpoint of a junior in high school, I wasn't too interested in the senior-class activities. I knew they were having a baccalaureate service on Sunday evening and one of the local ministers would be speaking. I had heard it would be the Methodist pastor this year. That was the church Carl and his family attended so he would be happy about that, I thought. They had already had their all-day trip away from the school. They had gone on the train to Topeka, the state capitol, and visited various places of interest there. Carl said he enjoyed getting to tour the capitol and meeting some of the legislators.

With only two weeks more of school, our last high-school assembly was announced for Friday at 2:00 p.m. All of us would be missing our last class of the day to attend. When we filed into the auditorium, I noticed that there were more school officials on the platform than usual. The school superintendent, Dr. Alderson, sat near the podium. We knew he would be reading the 13th chapter of I Corinthians from the Bible. He always did. "When I was a child I spoke as a child, but when I became a man I put away childish things." Today he would put more emphasis than usual on that portion because the seniors were being honored.

A whole section in the front of the auditorium was reserved for the seniors. Mary Ann and I were in agreement, "Oh, good, we can sit in the balcony today and look down at the boys." I really didn't like sitting in the balcony, though most of the kids did. I always felt being up so high was unreal and thought, *What if I went crazy and decided to jump?* That thought was never expressed to anyone aloud,

233

but I did think it and felt quite uncomfortable. I couldn't believe that some of the boys leaned way over the railing.

After we were all seated, the seniors filed in and took their assigned seats. They were introduced as a group, and some of those receiving special honors were named and asked to stand. We were expected to clap, but not for too long. The program was to be finished in time for dismissal at the regular time. As we expected, Dr. Alderson did read from the Bible. Then two of the senior boys who had won first place in the music meet played their trumpets.

It wasn't really a very long assembly because most of what was happening would be repeated at the graduation ceremonies in a week and a half. I saw Carl in the second row and wondered if he would look up into the balcony so I could smile at him, but he never did. After the program was over, the seniors were permitted to file out first before the rest of us were dismissed. Would I see as much of Carl the next year as I had the last? He did not plan to go to college right away and would be home helping his dad on the farm.

The first weekend after school was out, Carl and his entire family came over to our house one evening for a visit. Mother had baked a cake and served it with coffee. The parents all visited in the living room while the Jensen boys sat on the front porch with Dora Lynne, Edna June and me. We mostly talked about what everyone would be doing during the summer. As they got ready to leave, Carl's mother said, "I was wondering if Bonnie May could come to the farm for the weekend. We'd bring her home Sunday when we come in to church."

I was surprised at Mother's reaction. She wouldn't even consider it. She said, "No, she can't." No explanation. I started to argue, but decided I'd better not. That was one time I didn't understand my mother at all. I had thought it would be fun to spend the whole weekend with Carl, but that was not to be. There must have been something in my mother's background that frightened her at the thought of her firstborn daughter spending a whole weekend with a boy. I didn't try to figure it out, I just accepted the ultimatum. That is the way we were brought up.

CHAPTER FIFTEEN

HOPE FOR TOMORROW

Overseas, Hitler was systematically building up his air and ground forces and seizing land at every opportunity. Someone said he had grabbed just under 80,000 square miles for Germany. Little Austria had not had a chance against his greedy power. All the signals were there; But to most of us, Germany and Austria seemed far away. We weren't used to following events in Europe. Most of my life I had heard adults rather vaguely speak of the possibility of war, but events in our hometown in the middle of Kansas occupied our minds and lives. We were still feeling the results of a very severe economic depression. Nobody wanted to think about anything worse happening.

To most of us who were high-school seniors, war was not in our thoughts. All we really knew of war was from our history books and the few stories our parents had shared about World War I—"the war to end all wars."

My dad had never really talked much about the serious side of war. He often told a funny story about trying to communicate with the French or some other event when one of the soldiers had made an amusing remark. Actually, he had suffered a great deal from his experiences overseas. Mostly, the suffering was emotional.

One of the events of our senior year which occupied my mind was the preparation for giving the senior play. This year, it was to be *Little Women*. I loved the story and felt that I could truly identify with the character Jo. So, when it was announced that tryouts for the parts would be next Tuesday, I decided to try out for the part of Jo. I knew I could portray her well in spite of my tendency to have stage fright. Acting would be different.

All weekend I prayed that God would give me the part. Already I was imagining how the costumes would look. I'd seen pictures in one of the books I had read. My imagination embellished the pictures and I even practiced swishing around in a long gown. So far as being the oldest in the family and a bit bossy, that was just a part of my life. If I lived it, I could also portray it, I felt.

The day of tryouts finally came and it was difficult paying attention in class. I was thinking about what would take place in the gym after school. I could almost hear Miss Myers say, "Why, Bonnie, I didn't know you could act. You are perfect for the part."

When I walked into the gymnasium, I was surprised to see the number of seniors lined up to try out for parts.

At once, I spotted Alicia, a friend from the east end of town. Her parents were French and, for some reason, had wished her to attend public school instead of the parochial school which most of the French children attended. Even so, she had not been truly accepted by the rest of the students, especially the west-enders; but then, neither was I. I was somewhat on the fringes because of my cousin who was in the center of the west-end social circle. Occasionally, she was required to include me in her activities and the other girls didn't seem to mind.

I asked Alicia which part she intended to try out for and she hesitated a bit. "Well, I was hoping to try out for Meg, but then I decided I'd like to try for Beth. It is so sad that she has to die, but it would be a great opportunity to do some serious acting. And I have always intended to be an actress some day."

Our conversation was interrupted by Miss Myers who reminded us that we must hurry and complete the sign-up sheet indicating the part we wanted to play. Alicia and I soon took care of that little chore and joined the crowd to wait for further instructions. Alicia said, "I have goose bumps just thinking about it. Are you nervous?"

"Yes, a little," I admitted, "but that isn't going to stop me. I feel pretty certain about this. I have a special reason to be positive about getting the part." I didn't share any more with Alicia about praying and asking God to give me the part. She might not understand—not everyone believed in prayer. I was sure that Alicia did because she was Catholic and I knew most of them prayed a lot.

Miss Myers was trying to get our attention again. "Now, I want all those who have signed up for the various parts to meet together as I point out. The *Jo's* in that corner, the

Megs in this corner, The *mothers* here in front." And so on, until she had covered every part. There were a lot more Megs and Jo's than there were mothers, of course; and when it came to the one-line speaking parts, there weren't too many who wanted to do that.

After everyone had said the lines assigned to them, Miss Myers said, "The parts will be posted on the bulletin board tomorrow morning. Thank you all for trying out." And that was all. Walking home, I began to have some doubts. But I had prayed, hadn't I? And I knew the Bible said: *Ask and it shall be given you*, or something like that.

I didn't sleep much that night. I kept thinking about getting the part in the play, going on to bigger things— maybe Hollywood. Who knows? I might prove to this stuck-up little town that I could become someone. Why did there have to be "the right side" and "the wrong side" of town, anyway?

The first thing most of us did on arriving at school the next day was to go see the bulletin board just outside the principal's office. Opposite the name *Jo* was Martha Allen. I couldn't believe it. She wasn't right for the part at all. Then I looked down at *Meg* and opposite this was Kathryn Smythe, "Spelled with a 'K,' my dear." She always said so. I forced myself to look at the entire cast of characters. Neither Alicia's nor my name appeared anywhere. I felt devastated. Surely God had let me down.

Later that morning, on the way to English literature class, I met Alicia. She said, "I want to walk part way home with you today. I'm going in to talk to Miss Myers about those parts. She must have made a mistake somewhere."

I shrugged my shoulders, "It's up to you. I don't want anything to do with the stupid play."

On the way home, Alicia shared with me her conversation with Miss Myers. "She said that both you and I would have been good for the parts, but that she had no choice."

I was shocked at that remark, "No choice. How could that be? She is in charge of the whole production."

Alicia shook her head, "No, she said that she had been told by the principal that she must choose people from the west end because their fathers owned the businesses in town; and they would be contributing financially to the school to buy sets and costumes."

That was my first taste of small-town politics reaching down into my world, and I didn't like it. It just wasn't fair. Besides, I had prayed and I really trusted God to overrule any silly political preferences.

I didn't share my feelings with anyone but disappointment was there, and a bit of anger—mostly at God who had let me down. Well, I wasn't going to let it ruin my life. I knew there would be other opportunities to excel; probably in some other place, and hopefully in the not too distant future.

I had never allowed my position in life to keep me down for long. I combated the poverty with a strong and sometimes foolish pride. I was convinced that I could do almost anything. The real problem now was that, spiritually, I was not progressing. I wanted to use God to help me get there, and I couldn't see why He hadn't.

What really upset me was that Mother was asked to make the costumes for the play—all those romantic gowns. That was like pouring salt on my wounded feelings. I had hoped she would say no, but she wasn't struggling with pride and disappointment as I was. She said yes. We really needed the money.

The next week, another situation occurred to cause me to evaluate my relationship with God. I had become used to praying often. I disciplined myself to read one chapter from the Bible every day whether I understood it or not, then I would pray a long list of requests. This particular Saturday evening, Herbert had asked Dad for the car to take a group of his friends for a ride in the country. He had saved enough money to buy the gas. Dad gave him the car keys and said, "Drive carefully and don't stay out past 11:30." That was the time the folks usually set for us on a weekend night.

After I had read my chapter from the Bible that evening, I prayed my usual list of requests. I hadn't gotten used to saying "thank you." At the top of my list was a request for the safety of Herbert as he drove. I was always the worrier and could imagine all the terrible things that could happen if he had a wreck.

I went to bed rather early to read. Dora Lynne was snoring away already and didn't even notice that I had the light on. After an hour or so I drifted off to sleep and was later awakened by the sound of the telephone ringing. I heard the clock strike midnight. I was filled with foreboding. Something had happened.

I got out of bed and went into the kitchen where Daddy was talking on the telephone. I heard him say, "I'll be there as soon as I can get dressed and wake up the neighbor to bring me over."

"What happened?" I didn't really want to know. My mind was filled with visions of the worst kind, all concerning my brother. *Was he alive?*

Daddy explained that there had been a wreck on a country road, that all the young people were all right—a bit shaken up, but all right. The car would have to be towed in, of course, and repaired.

Again, I was accusing God. He had let me down. I offered in a hopeless tone, "But I prayed—"

Mother was very quick to set me straight, "And God answered. All the young people are safe. What is a car in comparison? God doesn't always answer our prayers in the way we think He should, but He always answers; and He has taken care of our Herbert tonight. Don't question God's wisdom. He knows what is best."

I took a giant step in my spiritual development that night. I learned how to say, "Thank you, God. You know best."

The matter of Herbert's accident furnished another look at small-town politics. Herbert had told us how the accident happened. He was driving along this country road when a car came speeding from behind, raced around them and pulled back in too soon. The driver of the other car was drunk. His car caught the front fender of our car, flipping it over in the ditch. Ours was an old touring sedan which had a cloth top. All of the boys and girls in our car were thrown through the top of the car. Fortunately, they were all thrown clear and were not seriously hurt. The other driver didn't even stop.

Daddy said he thought he'd better go talk to Benny Hart, one of our local attorneys. The other driver should at least have to pay for the repairs of our car. When he came home after visiting with Mr. Hart, he just shook his head. "No, that other driver is the son of Aaron Kincaid, the banker, and Mr. Hart said there would be no way we could get anything out of them. Going to court would be too expensive and the judge probably would not hear anything against the Kincaids."

Talk about unfair. I had grown rather accustomed to it. That's just the way things were and if you were poor there wasn't much chance of changing them. I decided I might just try someday to beat the system, but it surely wouldn't be in Bentley. Maybe things were more fair somewhere else.

Anyway, I had to get on with being a senior in high school and making plans for life after high school. That year, the government was giving some aid to needy students in the form of jobs at the school. I signed up for the assistance and, because of my business education, was given the job of keeping the records for all working students. I would record the hours they worked and figure the amount they were to be paid. It was an easy job and only took a few hours each week. Also, I was allowed to help in the cafeteria. For that, most of the time, I received a free lunch but no pay.

One day Mother said Mrs. Burkhart had called. I didn't know her, but Mother said she was a lady who lived in the west end, had a lovely home and maintained a florist shop in the back part of her home. She wanted someone to come in two afternoons a week after school just to answer the telephone. She must have gotten my name from the school. She would pay a small amount each time. I agreed it would be a good way to make a little more money.

The next afternoon, I went over to see Mrs. Burkhart and receive instructions. She seemed to approve of me and said she would pay me fifty cents an afternoon. It was a great opportunity and I promised to return the next day to start work. It really wasn't work. I could do homework, read, listen to her radio, or just sit and dream. I often pretended to be older and own a beautiful home like the one I was in. But, of course, I would decorate it in my own way; and there never would be a shortage of anything. I'd have candy dishes around, lots of fresh flowers in every room, rare paintings on the walls—I could dream as much as I wanted because it was certainly a do-nothing kind of job.

I think most of all I liked the peace and quiet, something we seldom had around our house with so many children. If the phone rang, I was to answer: "Mrs. Burkhart's Flowers." It never rang in the entire eight months I worked for her. I didn't know if this was just a hobby with her or if she actually hoped to make some money. I thought of ways she could improve business by doing some simple advertising but never got up nerve enough to speak to her about it.

I remember that I was always cold in the winter. Kansas winters can be very severe, and my blood must have been thin because I never seemed to warm up until spring. Mrs. Burkhart had a furnace with a thermostat. I had never even seen a thermostat. She explained that if I needed more heat I could turn up the thermostat.

That was just what I wanted. Each day, as soon as she left, I turned up the thermostat and left it up until a half hour before she returned. Then I turned it down. Rather dishonest of me, of course, but I was so glad to be really warm I didn't let my conscience get in the way.

I was becoming so fast in shorthand and so accurate in typing that Miss Cromwell seemed to be quite impressed. I achieved several awards given by the Gregg company. Miss Cromwell had been a student of John R. Gregg, so I was certain she was the best teacher I could have. She had wanted me to take bookkeeping from her, but I had balked at the idea. Any kind of figures made me extremely nervous. I think it stemmed from my early difficulty with arithmetic. I probably was not willing to make the effort to improve.

One day, Miss Cromwell asked me to stay after school for a few minutes. When I walked in she said, "Sit down, Miss J. I want to talk to you." She was always rather stern and some of the students were afraid of her. I respected her, but I wasn't actually afraid of her. I knew she was a serious teacher who wanted every one of her students to succeed in the business world. She was well known for weeding out from each of her classes at the beginning of the year, getting the less serious students to drop the class. I don't know how she did it, but she always did. She taught a small, tight-knit group of students, each determined to be excellent.

"I know you didn't show much interest last year when I suggested that you prepare for college." Actually, I had taken two years of Latin which met the language requirement. I might have needed another math class, but didn't consider college an option anyway.

She went on, "But you know you could go far in the business world and I'd like to see you attend the state university. I have friends there who could get work for you and you could probably get a loan or grant for the tuition. Would you consider it?"

I hesitated. It was exciting even to consider going to college. None in our family had a college degree. In fact, Mother and Daddy did not have high-school diplomas. Getting that diploma was the goal I had set for myself and I was sure that neither of my parents had planned beyond a high-school education for any of their children. Both of them were rather eager to see me get a job in town and help the family with expenses.

I might as well be honest. There really was no use thinking about it. "Well, I am sure I would enjoy going to college. Maybe later. Right now I have to finish high school and see about going to work. My folks really need my help."

Miss Cromwell may have been disappointed, but she honored my decision. She offered, "I know you must have thought it over. Now, as to getting a job, you won't have any trouble on that score. Any business in town will hire a student of mine." She was proud of her reputation and I was proud to have been her student. I was determined not to let her down no matter where I went to work.

One of the most exciting days of the senior year was Ditch Day. It was approved, planned and supervised by the school. This year we would be going on an overnight train trip to Kansas City, Missouri. The trip itself would be fun. We would leave the station very early, about 4:00 a.m., spend the day in K.C. visiting various places of interest and then start back home in the evening. It would be after midnight when we arrived home. None of us had ever done anything so unorthodox and the anticipation was high.

I got to sit beside Tony Thomas, a boy whom I knew quite well from being at his table in study hall. We had sometimes studied together. His older brother had graduated the year before. Their mother was a widow and had brought up both boys to be friendly and very polite. I didn't ever consider him more than a friend but occasionally thought it would be nice if he would ask me for a date. He never did.

As we toured Kansas City on a bus which the school had rented, we had a great time singing and laughing.

247

There were no status barriers that day. The west-end kids and the east-end kids for once seemed to be equal, with everyone kidding with everyone else. Funny what one common-interest day could accomplish.

One of the places we visited was the meat-packing plant. I don't know why the "powers that be" had thought we needed to see that, but Kansas City was known for its meat-packing plants. They took us through the area where the little calves were lined up to be sacrificed for veal meals. I'll admit that before this I hadn't known where veal came from. Before the day was over I wished I could have remained ignorant.

There was a small gate through which the calves were pushed one at a time. A huge black man stood inside the next small enclosure with a large mallet in his hand. He smashed the skull of that calf and another man slit its throat. Then the carcass was thrown onto a belt which took it to the next destination. Fortunately, we weren't required to stay and watch much of this performance, but I felt rather sick as we walked out into the clean, fresh outdoors.

The next stop was a beautiful park for a picnic lunch. I didn't enjoy the meal because I had trouble getting the picture of those helpless little calves out of my mind. I have always loved any babies, be they human or animal, and it just didn't seem right. Veal is not one of my favorite kinds of meat. Of course, we couldn't afford much meat anyway; so I decided that whatever they make hamburger out of, the procedure must be more humane.

The train trip home was as much fun as the day's activities. Everyone was tired, of course. A few were falling asleep. Most, however, were still wide-eyed and talking over the day's events. Tony began to sing "On the Road to Mandalay." He had a very good voice. Others joined and, before long, suggestions for the next song were flying all over the train. We all sang, whether we had good voices or not.

I had always been self-conscious about my singing voice. So to make up for it, I had joined Girls Glee Club that year. I must not have messed up the performances too much because we won first place at the county meet and went on to the state meet. We didn't win anything there.

One day the music teacher told me that she was making up a girls' trio and would like for me to try out for it. The idea petrified me. I stammered, "I don't think so." I wouldn't even try out for fear the embarrassment would be overwhelming. I came to the conclusion that teacher must not have been listening very closely to me when I sang.

The school year was winding down and everyone was telling what their plans were for after graduation. Ginny Patterson said she was going to college, of course. She was kind of on the fringe of the west-enders since her father was a small-business man in town. She was a very pretty girl and had been chosen for the homecoming queen that year. She got to ride on a float in the homecoming parade and had special recognition at the last football game of the year.

My cousin, Barbara Jean, told us that she had to go to college, too. She intended to become a schoolteacher. Since her parents could afford to send her to college, she wouldn't have to work while attending.

Tony was planning to enlist in the navy. His brother had already enlisted and he was hoping they could be on a ship together after he finished his training. It was rather unnerving that several of the boys were enlisting for the service. They felt they would be drafted anyway. There was some talk of war, and patriotism was running high. I didn't like it. I thought if we would disregard the situation "over there" it would go away on its own. That was a narrow view, but I was comfortable with it.

Pauline Kingsley said she and a friend planned to go to California. She said she knew she could get work of some kind out there; and, after all, who wanted to stay in Bentley forever? I agreed with her on that point but didn't see how I could ever voluntarily leave my parents unless I were getting married.

One day, Daddy said he had some exciting news. He had talked to Andy Longmeir who worked for the local loan company. Daddy was very familiar with those who worked for the loan company, I think because he had often used their services. It was rather outrageous the amount of interest that company charged; and most of its clients were the very poor, like my father. Daddy told Andy that I was graduating and would be looking for an office job soon. Andy talked to his boss and reported to Daddy that they would be hiring another girl soon. I was to go in and talk with them. I did and was hired to start work the week after school ended.

I was elated. It made me feel so important to know I was to be a working girl. The pay wasn't anything to brag about, but the working conditions were quite pleasant. Two other girls worked in the office and would be training me. I immediately liked both of them and looked forward to beginning work.

As the end of the school year approached, I was surprised to receive a number of gifts. I didn't know one received gifts for graduation. Mrs. Burkhart sent me a beautiful lingerie set. I had never had underwear like it in all my life. Mrs. Hanson from church gave me a book on missions. There was also perfume and a pretty little picture frame—better than Christmas!

One more week to graduation! I could hardly wait. It was a milestone that I had been anticipating for several years. The plans and preparations were on everyone's mind. We seniors had to check out our caps and gowns, and sit through instructions on what to do when we arrived at the auditorium—where each of us would sit, alphabetically, of course. We practiced walking up the aisle, standing on the platform, receiving our diplomas and going back to our seats. The speakers had been assigned and told where they would stand and how long they were to talk.

As soon as I took my cap and gown home, I tried them on and Herbert said, "Come on outside, I borrowed a friend's camera." So there was a great deal of posing, clicking and laughter all around. I felt like a movie star.

Just before we left for the graduation ceremonies, a lovely corsage arrived from Mrs. Burkhart. *How thoughtful of her.* The whole family attended graduation, even little Anne Louise. I was a bit embarrassed that there were so many of them. Then I felt guilty about being embarrassed. They all behaved very well, sat quietly and did nothing to further embarrass me beyond just being there—and being so numerous.

The valedictorian was such an intelligent boy. His parents owned a furniture store in town, but he never lorded it over any of the other students. He wasn't very popular with the boys, possibly because he was such a good student and didn't enter into sports.

The real heroes in class were the football players. No matter where they lived, they managed to go with all the popular west-end girls. Herbert was on the team and was included in many of the social events because of that. I think he was always trying to prove his own worth, just as I was. Neither of us liked the social stratification of our small town. We knew there was more to life than which end of the town you lived in and what your father did for a living.

Mr. Alderson, the superintendent of schools, opened the graduation ceremony with prayer. Surprisingly, he didn't read the 13th chapter of I Corinthians, as he almost always did at assemblies. He did, however, give a little speech on how proud he was of the graduating class and how much he expected them to achieve in the future.

After Mr. Alderson's speech, the honors students were named and the valedictorian was introduced. He had a very good speech on the opportunities that lay ahead for all of us no matter what field of endeavor we pursued. He closed by saying that each of us must remember that our integrity would be on the line every day of our lives. We would have to make choices and they could be either good or bad, depending on what we wanted out of life. The most important thing, he said, was always to be totally honest—with others and with ourselves.

There was a girls' trio which sang a number they had practiced in the glee club for the last six months. Then the keynote speaker, a man from a neighboring town, gave the speech which was meant to encourage and motivate us to go out and win the world. He said, "Remember, you can be anyone you want to be. You, young man, young woman, are this world's hope for tomorrow. You can do anything you want to do. Now go out and do it."

I wasn't sure just how that pertained to me, but I did feel somewhat challenged, thinking, *I really can be anyone I want to be. Now, if I just knew what that was.*

After we marched up to receive our diplomas, Dr. Allen, an Episcopalian priest in town, gave the benediction. We left the auditorium in high spirits.

I saw Barbara Jean in the middle of a circle of her west-end friends. They were all squealing, laughing and hugging one another. She didn't even see me. I met my friend, Mary Ann, at the door and said, "Well, we made it."

She smiled, "Yes, we did."

Outside the school, I saw the family crowding into our car. I told them I thought I would walk home, and Daddy said, "All right, if you want to. We'll see you soon."

It was a moonlit, starry night and I enjoyed the solitude as I walked slowly home. I wanted a little time with my thoughts. I hadn't known much of life outside of school. Thinking about getting up in the mornings and going to work was totally new, and I wasn't sure how fulfilling that was going to be. But it would be different—no more government shoes. I could soon buy my own.

My thoughts rambled on. I had dreamed about this night. It was to have been the happiest time of my life because I had finally completed my education. Somehow, though, I felt a tremendous letdown. There must be more for me out there in the real world. Perhaps I shouldn't be so quick to dream a dream, even if the possibilities were unlimited. Perhaps I should learn to live in the real world.

I knew that for a while I would be working for the loan company. I'd be helping the family buy groceries. I would always buy my own shoes. But there just had to be more.

I longed to leave Bentley, to go on to something bigger and better. I was convinced that someday I would get away from the small town with its petty politics. However, for the present, I must put aside the restlessness.

Just then, our house came into view and I could see the lights on in every room, hear the good-natured bantering of my siblings, a radio playing somewhere, Mother calling, "Anne Louise, come get ready for bed."

Now, that is reality! For now, it is enough. Tomorrow...who knows?

To order additional copies of
Tomorrow's Troubles
send $11.99 + $3.95 shipping and handling to:

WinePress Publishing
PO Box 1406
Mukilteo, WA 98275

•

To order by phone
have your credit card ready and call:

(800) 917–BOOK